MIDDLE EAST NATIONS IN THE NEWS

Turkey IN THE NEWS

PAST, PRESENT, AND FUTURE

Christine Kohler

MyReportLinks.com Books
an imprint of
Enslow Publishers, Inc.
Box 398, 40 Industrial Road
Berkeley Heights, NJ 07922
USA

MyReportLinks.com Books, an imprint of Enslow Publishers, Inc. MyReportLinks®
is a registered trademark of Enslow Publishers, Inc.

Library of Congress Cataloging-in-Publication Data

Kohler, Christine, 1953–
Turkey in the news : past, present, and future / Christine Kohler.
p. cm. — (Middle East nations in the news)
Includes bibliographical references and index.
ISBN 1-59845-024-7
1. Turkey—Juvenile literature. 2. Turkey—History—Juvenile literature. 3. Turkey—Social conditions—Juvenile literature. 4. Turkey—Economic conditions—Juvenile literature. I. Title. II. Series.
DR417.K64 2006
956.1—dc22
2005018762

Printed in the United States of America

10 9 8 7 6 5 4 3 2 1

To Our Readers:
Through the purchase of this book, you and your library gain access to the Report Links that specifically back up this book.
The Publisher will provide access to the Report Links that back up this book and will keep these Report Links up to date on **www.myreportlinks.com** for five years from the book's first publication date.
We have done our best to make sure all Internet addresses in this book were active and appropriate when we went to press. However, the author and the Publisher have no control over, and assume no liability for, the material available on those Internet sites or on other Web sites they may link to.
The usage of the MyReportLinks.com Books Web site is subject to the terms and conditions stated on the Usage Policy Statement on **www.myreportlinks.com.**
A password may be required to access the Report Links that back up this book. The password is found on the bottom of page 4 of this book.
Any comments or suggestions can be sent by e-mail to comments@myreportlinks.com or to the address on the back cover.

Photo Credits: © 1995–2005 istanbul.com, p. 42; © 2000 The British Museum, p. 59; © 2001–2005 FIFA; © 2002 Time Inc., p. 95; © 2003–5 Arizona Board of Regents, p. 20; © 2005 REPUBLIC OF TURKEY MINISTRY OF CULTURE AND TOURISM, p. 40; © 2005 WN Network, p. 15; © Burak Sansal 1996–2005, p. 56; © Copyright 2002 Heights Productions, Inc./Public Broadcasting Service (PBS), p. 106; © Corel Corporation, pp. 3, 26, 36, 50, 65, 67, 94, 99; ©1996, Richard Hooker, p. 70; © Turkey TravelPlanner.com, p. 39; AP/Wide World Photos, pp. 10, 16, 114; Ataturk.com, p. 83; British Broadcasting Corporation © 2002–2005, pp. 12, 48, 89; Central Intelligence Agency (CIA), p. 72; Copyright © 1996–2005 United Nations, p. 91; Copyright © 1997 Serif Yenen, p. 79; Copyright © 2002 United Nations, p. 111; Copyright © 2003 Embassy of the Republic of Turkey, Washington, DC, p. 24; Copyright © 2004 Ministry of Foreign Affairs, Balgat 06100 Ankara – Turkey, p. 85; Copyright © 2004 Thomas G. Hines, Department of Theatre, Whitman College, p. 49; Copyright © 2005 Aramco Services Company, pp. 30, 33, 45, 52, 81, 101; Copyright Lee Krystek 1998, p. 63; Courtesy of the University of Texas Libraries, The University of Texas at Austin, pp. 46, 112; Enslow Publishers, Inc., p. 5; EPA photo/Kerim Okten, pp. 28, 87; EPA photo/Tarik Tinazay, p. 103; EUROPA, p. 109; Library of Congress, pp. 74, 97; Ministry of Culture and Tourism, Turkey, p. 22; MyReportLinks.com Books, p. 4; NATO, p. 6; Photos.com, pp. 58, 86, 108; turkeyinmaps.com, p. 62; Türkiye Büyük Millet Meclisi, p. 93; U.S. State Department, p. 76.

Cover Photo: AP/Wide World Photos

Cover Description: A child holds a balloon decorated with the Turkish emblem, right, and a balloon decorated with the emblem of the European Union, left. This child is one in a crowd showing their support for Turkey's desire to enter the EU.

Contents

About MyReportLinks.com Books 4
Map 5
Turkey Facts 6
Time Line 7
1 **Terrorism in Turkey** 9
2 **Land, Water, and Climate** 18
3 **Islam** 27
4 **Culture** 38
5 **Ancient Peoples** 59
6 **Twentieth-Century Turkey** 78
7 **Economy** 97
8 **Challenges of the Future** 107
Report Links 116
Glossary 118
Chapter Notes 120
Further Reading 125
Index 126

Fishing along the Bosporus

Cappadocia

MyReportLinks.com Books

Great Books, Great Links, Great for Research!

The Internet sites featured in this book can save you hours of research time. These Internet sites—we call them **"Report Links"**—are constantly changing, but we keep them up to date on our Web site.

When you see this "Approved Web Site" logo, you will know that we are directing you to a great Internet site that will help you with your research.

Give it a try! Type http://www.myreportlinks.com into your browser, click on the series title and enter the password, then click on the book title, and scroll down to the Report Links listed for this book.

The Report Links will bring you to great source documents, photographs, and illustrations. MyReportLinks.com Books save you time, feature Report Links that are kept up to date, and make report writing easier than ever! A complete listing of the Report Links can be found on pages 116–117 at the back of the book.

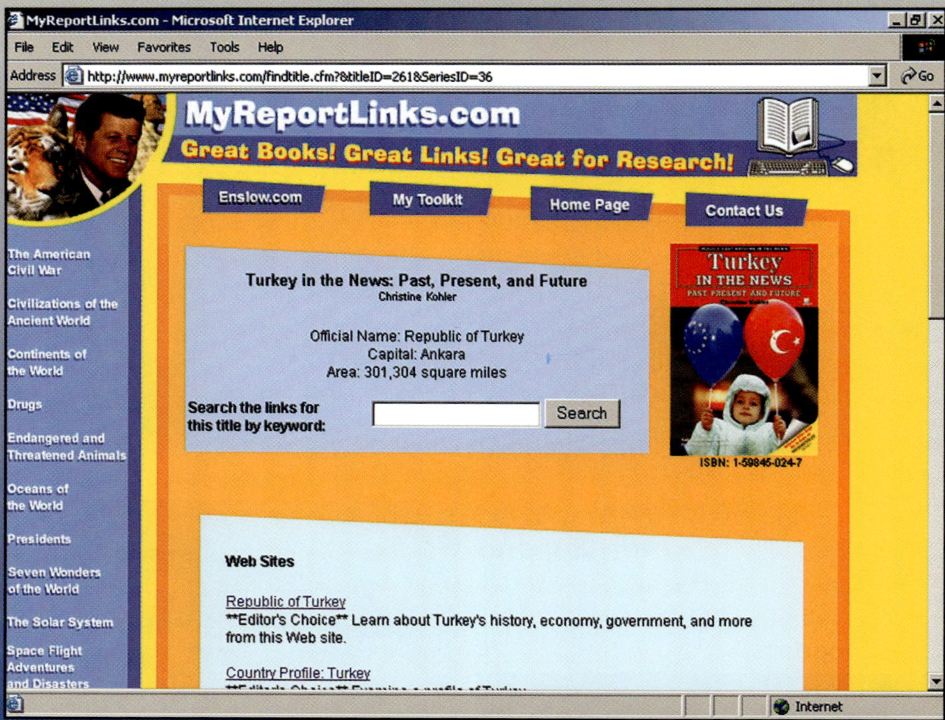

Please see "To Our Readers" on the copyright page for important information about this book, the MyReportLinks.com Web site, and the Report Links that back up this book.

Please enter **NTU1369** if asked for a password.

A map of present-day Turkey.

Turkey Facts

Flag
A white vertical crescent and five-pointed star on a red background

Capital
Ankara

Population
69,660,559 (July 2005 estimate)

Area
297,592 square miles

Highest Point
Mount Ararat, 16,949 feet

Lowest Point
Mediterranean Sea, sea level

President Sezer of Turkey

Location
Southwestern Asia (97 percent) and southeastern Europe (3 percent)

Type of Government
Republican parliamentary democracy

Head of State
President Ahmet Necdet Sezer

Head of Government
Prime Minister Recep Tayyip Erdogan

Monetary Unit
New Turkish lira

Official Language
Turkish

National Anthem
"March of Independence"

Religion
Muslim (mostly Sunni—99.8 percent), other (mostly Christian and Jewish—0.2 percent)

National Holiday
Republic Day (October 29)

Time Line

23,000 B.C.—The Karain cave becomes home to humans. It is one of the earliest known settlements in Anatolia.

1269 B.C. —After battling, King Moursil of the Hittites and Pharaoh Ramses of Egypt sign one of history's earliest known peace agreements.

547 B.C. —Persian king Cyrus Achaemenid conquers Anatolia, making the area part of the Persian Empire.

334 B.C. —Anatolia is conquered by Alexander the Great.

63 B.C. —The Romans take control of Anatolia.

A.D. 330 —Emperor Constantine the Great shifts the capital of the Roman Empire from Rome to Byzantium, which is renamed Constantinople in his honor.

1071–1171—Seljuk leader Alp Arslan leads Turkish gazis to defeat the Byzantine Army, taking control of Anatolia.

1189–92 —King Richard the Lionheart places Anatolia under English control during the Third Crusade.

1291 —The Ottoman Turks rise to power in Anatolia.

1919–22 —Foreign troops occupy Ottoman territories following World War I. The Turks resist, leading to the War of Independence.

1920 —*August 10:* The Ottoman Empire is forced to sign the Treaty of Sèvres.

1922 —*November 1:* The office of sultan is abolished by the Grand National Assembly, thereby ending the Ottoman Empire.

1923 —*October 29:* A new Turkish state, the Republic of Turkey, is formed. Mustafa Kemal Pasha is voted president.

1928 —*April 10:* Turkey is declared a secular state.

1938 —*November 10:* Mustafa Kemal Atatürk dies.

1960 —*May 27:* An army coup takes over the government.

1980 —*September 12:* Political disagreements lead to a military coup. Martial law is imposed.

1982 —*July 17:* Turkey's most recent constitution is drafted.

1983 —*November 15:* Turkish Cypriots declare themselves a separate state. The United Nations (UN) declares this succession illegal.

1999 —*December 10–11:* Turkey officially becomes a candidate for European Union (EU) membership.

2005 —*October 3:* The EU formally begins membership talks with Turkey.

Chapter 1 ▶

Terrorism in Turkey

Thirteen-year-old Aaron Cohen studied Hebrew and the Torah for years. On November 15, 2003, Aaron and about three hundred of his family and friends gathered to celebrate Aaron's bar mitzvah at Neve Shalom Synagogue in Istanbul. Neve Shalom, which in Hebrew means "oasis of peace," is the largest synagogue in Turkey.

Aaron must have been excited and anxious at such an important milestone in his life. A bar mitzvah is a solemn and holy ceremony where a young male is initiated into the Jewish community. Aaron and the rabbi rose to their feet. The congregation also stood up. Aaron was about to chant in Hebrew his bar mitzvah reading from the Torah.[1] This would be his first act as a man, according to Jewish tradition.

All of a sudden, a loud explosion went off, causing the synagogue roof to shatter. Showers of broken glass rained down on the people in Neve Shalom. The explosion from a bomb in an Isuzu

Investigators examine the damage caused by suicide car bombers outside of Neve Shalom Synagogue. Earlier that day, November 15, 2003, the bombers blew up their Isuzu truck in front of the Jewish house of worship. The blast killed twenty-two people.

truck blew a huge crater in the street in front of the synagogue.

Another Synagogue Targeted

Three miles away at almost the same time—about 10:00 A.M.—terrorists struck. They rammed another Isuzu truck into Beth Israel Synagogue. The truck had been packed with 880 pounds of explosives.[2]

In all, twenty-two people died at Neve Shalom. Three people died at Beth Israel. About 260 people were wounded altogether. Most of the people dead and hurt were Muslims. Among the dead were Aaron's cousin, Berta Ozdogan, and her husband, Ahmet. Berta was pregnant with their first child. Berta and Ahmet were both buried in coffins draped with Turkish flags. However, they could not be buried in the same cemetery, for Ahmet was Muslim.[3]

Neve Shalom's Rabbi Isak Haleva commented, "To do something like this when people are praying, this is truly beyond the pale of human conduct. Even animals don't commit evil like this."[4]

British Embassy and HSBC Bombings

Five days later, on November 20, a pickup truck packed with explosives crashed into the eighteen-story HSBC bank's Turkish headquarters located in Istanbul. The HSBC London-owned bank is the world's second largest bank.

BBC News: Middle East

Read all the latest news from the Middle East at this BBC Web site.

Access this Web site from http://www.myreportlinks.com

About five to ten minutes later, approximately six miles away, British Consul General Roger Short stepped back into his office. He had just gotten a quick shoe shine.[5] Meanwhile, his wife was in a café across the narrow street. She had gone to get her husband milk for his coffee.[6] Within that time, what looked like a food delivery truck smashed through the front wrought-iron gates of the British consulate.

Two Turkish guards shot at the truck and sounded an alarm. The truck exploded in the front of the consulate. Yellow smoke filled the air. The homemade bombs ripped apart buildings and a wall surrounding the consulate's garden. Cars, glass, blood, and bodies were scattered everywhere. Both guards and Roger Short died.

The explosions at HSBC and the British consulate killed at least 32 people and hurt nearly 450 people. Most of the dead were Turkish citizens.[7]

Terrorist Suspects

A group called Islamic Great Eastern Raiders' Front claimed they bombed the synagogues, British consulate, and HSBC bank headquarters. This group wants to overthrow the secular, or non-religious, Turkish government and replace it with a Sunni Islamic republic. Experts said, however, that the bombings were too sophisticated to have been carried out by the Great Eastern Raiders' Front. This terrorist group is small in comparison to others, and it is not well organized. Furthermore, the group's leader is in prison. For these reasons, experts did not think that group carried out the attacks. They believed that in order to create a terrifying image, the group claimed to be responsible for attacks carried out by other groups.[8]

British antiterrorist police teamed up with Turkish police and secret service men to investigate the bombings. They found that the Turkish men whom they arrested as well as one of the suicide bombers had been trained by al-Qaeda.

Al-Qaeda is an anti-Western network that funds and trains Islamic terrorists.

One captured al-Qaeda militant confessed that the group's target of choice was a Turkish military base used by the United States in southern Turkey. However, very tight security convinced the group to choose other Western and Jewish targets.[9] Al-Qaeda members believe they are carrying out the will of Allah by waging war against non-Muslims. In particular, they attack people from the United States and Israel. This holy war is called *jihad.*

Altogether, law enforcement officials accused seventy-one Turks with involvement in the four bombings. However, only thirty-eight people are being held in jail.[10]

Aftermath

Immediately after the attack on the HSBC bank in Istanbul, security was tightened at Jewish, Christian, American, and British sites in Istanbul. In addition, nearly one hundred Turkish troops guarded the area. The troops later withdrew.

Turkey's stock market started falling after the attacks. The stock exchange closed minutes later and remained closed the next day. Turkey had been recovering from a bad economic recession. Government officials feared tourists would be scared off from visiting Turkey and that foreign investors might be afraid to invest in Turkish businesses.[11]

Several countries, including Britain, warned citizens not to travel to Turkey. European soccer officials postponed international games in the country. Some Israeli tourists canceled vacations to Turkey.

In the midst of all this suffering, people reached out to the victims of the terrorism. Christ Church, where Roger Short and his wife attended church in Istanbul, set up a fund to help support widows and orphans whose wage-earning family members died in the blasts. HSBC officials donated one million dollars and took up a worldwide collection to support families hurt by the blast and pay for the advanced education of orphans as well

Turkey Observer

This site provides updated news articles from Turkey and the rest of the world.

EDITOR'S CHOICE

Access this Web site from http://www.myreportlinks.com

as the medical bills of staff members hurt in the bombing. Another fund was set up to help small local businesses that were damaged. Members of the Euro-Asian Jewish Congress invited Aaron Cohen and his family to complete his bar mitzvah ceremony at the Wailing Wall in Jerusalem, Israel. Instead, Aaron completed his bar mitzvah ceremony on March 13, 2004, at the Ceylan Intercontinental Hotel in Istanbul, Turkey.

A pedestrian walks past a memorial for those who lost their lives in the 2003 bombings of Neve Shalom, Beth Israel, the HSBC bank, and the British consulate. Located in front of what was once the Turkish headquarters of HSBC bank, the memorial banner translates to "It won't ever be forgotten!"

Rebuilding the Synagogues

After the bombings, most of Istanbul's synagogues stayed closed for a year or more. The Jewish people had to raise money and sometimes find new locations to build safer synagogues.

Finally, on October 11, 2004, Neve Shalom reopened with an official ceremony attended by political and civic leaders. Hundreds of Turkish Jews chanted hymns. A religious leader blew a ram's horn, sounding the call to worship. Torah scrolls rescued from Europe during World War II's holocaust of the Jews were donated to Neve Shalom.

Muslim and Christian religious leaders joined the Jews in their ceremony.

"This is a happy day and important day for us all," Emmanuel Nahshon, from the Israeli Embassy, said after the reopening ceremony of Neve Shalom. "This proves that the terrorists lost."[12]

Beth Israel reopened two months later in December 2004.

Land, Water, and Climate

Turkey sits at the crossroads where East meets West, and Africa lies to the south. Turkey's unique location is why kingdoms from both Asia and Europe have conquered it. It is because of this location that Turkey has become a blend of cultures and alliances.

Borders

Turkey is a rectangular peninsula located partly in Asia and partly in Europe. The Asian part of the country is the size of Texas. The European part is the size of Massachusetts. Eight countries border Turkey. On the Asian side lie Syria, Iraq, Iran, Armenia, Azerbaijan, and Georgia. Turkey sits on the European peninsula next to Bulgaria and Greece. Although the European peninsula makes up only 3 percent of Turkey's land, 10 percent of its population lives there.[1]

Turkey's coastline is about 4,474 miles long. Six bodies of water surround the peninsula on three sides. The Black Sea is to the north. The Bosporus strait is like a channel that links the Black Sea to the Sea of Marmara. The Dardanelles strait connects the Sea of Marmara to the Aegean Sea. To the south lies the Mediterranean Sea. The Mediterranean Sea is twice as salty as the Black Sea.

Mountains

The Asian part of Turkey was once called Asia Minor. Today it is called the Anatolia, which refers to the large, semiarid central plateau that covers the area. Hills and mountains surround this plateau.

More than 80 percent of Turkey's land is rough, broken, and mountainous. This limits how much land can be used for farming. Most of the mountains in Turkey are part of the great Alpine belt that extends from the Atlantic Ocean to the Himalaya Mountains.

The Taurus Mountains lie in southern Turkey. Mount Ararat (also called Agri Dagi), the country's highest peak, rises to 16,949 feet. It is situated in the Anti-Taurus Mountains near the point where four countries meet: Turkey, Armenia, Azerbaijan, and Iran. Mount Ararat is where the Torah and Bible say that Noah's ark landed when the Great Flood waters went down. August is the only month people can climb to the summit of Mount Ararat. The top is covered with snow and ice the rest of the year.

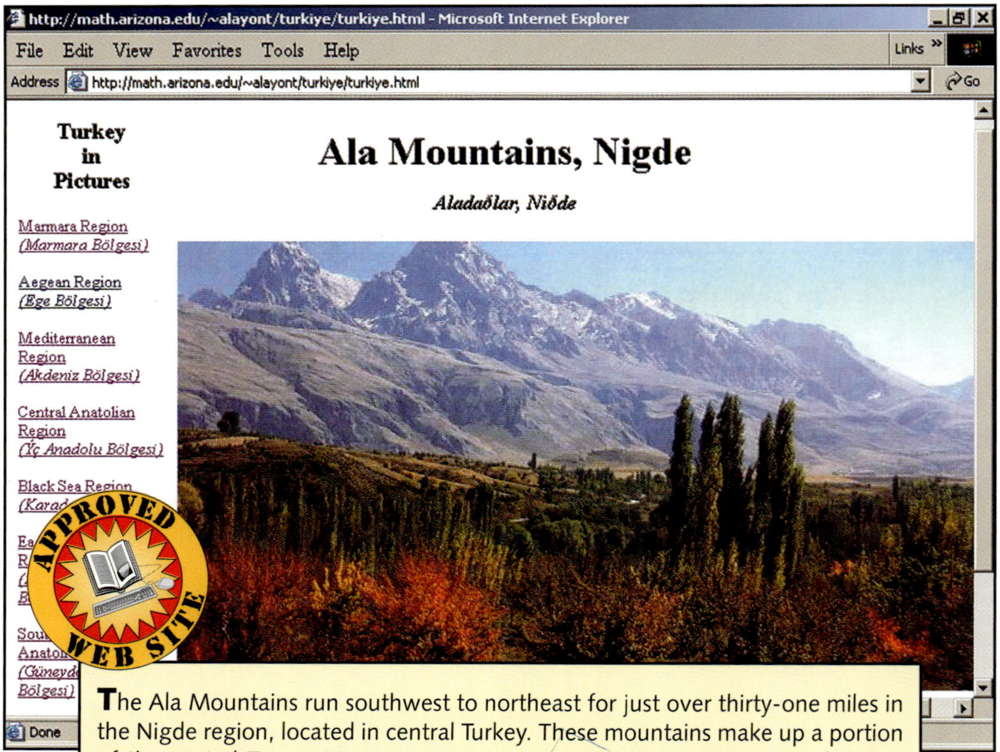

The Ala Mountains run southwest to northeast for just over thirty-one miles in the Nigde region, located in central Turkey. These mountains make up a portion of the central Taurus Mountains. You can view more scenic images of Turkey from the **Turkey in Pictures** Web site.

Lakes and Rivers

Turkey's largest lake, Lake Van, sits in the Anti-Taurus Mountains in the eastern part of the country. The second largest lake in Turkey is Lake Tuz. It lies within the two largest basins on the Central Anatolian Plateau. Lake Tuz is shallow and very salty.

Most of Turkey's rivers flow into the seas surrounding the peninsula. The Euphrates (also called Firat) and Tigris (known also as Dicle) begin in the highlands of Anatolia. In spring, when the snows melt, the rivers often flood. The Euphrates and Tigris rivers join together in Iraq. They flow into the Persian Gulf. This area is considered the Fertile Crescent and the "cradle of civilization." In both the Torah and the Bible, the Euphrates and Tigris are two of the rivers named as surrounding the Garden of Eden. The Garden of Eden is where religious books say the first man and woman, Adam and Eve, lived.

Turkey's longest rivers, the Kizil Irmak, Yesil Irmak, and Sakarya, flow into the Black Sea. The Seyhan, Ceyhan, and Göksu rivers empty into the Mediterranean Sea. The Maritsa (Meriç) River flows into the Aegean Sea. This river forms a natural border between Turkey and Greece.

Black Sea

Turkey is divided into seven regions: the Black Sea, Marmara, Aegean, Central Anatolia, East and Southeast Anatolia, and Mediterranean.[2] The Black Sea region has a steep, rocky coast. Rivers flow through the gorges of the coastal ranges. The Pontus Mountains stretch in the north like a wall along the Black Sea coast. There are only a few narrow valleys where people can pass through to get to the interior of Turkey. The higher slopes facing northwest are covered with dense forests.

The coast along the Black Sea is mild and damp. This makes for ideal growing conditions.

As in ancient times, the Mediterranean Sea is still used to transport goods from different nations. However, it is now also a popular tourist attraction. Fethiye, shown here, has some of the country's most beautiful beaches, and it is known for yachting. Learn more about Turkey's tourist areas from the **Turkey Welcomes You** Web site.

Farmers grow tobacco and citrus fruit on several narrow delta strips there.

Near the Black Sea the annual rainfall reaches up to more than one hundred inches.

Marmara

The Marmara region covers the area that circles the Sea of Marmara. This region includes the entire European portion of Turkey. It also includes the northwest Anatolian plain. Both the Asian and European banks rise steeply from the water. The banks form cliffs, coves, and nearly landlocked bays. Dense woods line the shores.

Aegean

The Aegean region, located on the western coast of Turkey, straddles the European and Asian sides of Turkey.

The European side is mainly a rolling plateau. It is good farmland. On the Asian side, the soil is also rich for farming. There are several important valleys and basins, including the Plains of Troy. There the ancient city of Troy is buried in nine layers, one on top of the others. The first city of Troy dates back to about 3000 to 2400 B.C. The Troy that Homer wrote about in *The Iliad* existed in about 1200 B.C.

The Aegean coasts have a Mediterranean climate of hot, dry summers and mild, wet winters.

Central Anatolia

The Central Anatolia region of Turkey contains the arid, steppe-like Anatolian Plateau. The plateau highlands make up the country's heartland. Basins caused by limestone erosion dot the land. Only the northeast and northwest sides of the plateau are wooded.

In the north, the Pontus Mountains (also called the North Anatolian Mountains) form an interrupted chain of folded highlands. Most of the Pontus Mountains parallel the Black Sea coastline.

Once thought a myth, the ancient city of Troy is now believed to have existed in present-day Hisarlik, Turkey. The poet Homer told of the Trojan Horse, a giant, wooden horse that held Greek warriors sneaking into Troy. Turkey's embassy in Washington, D.C., provides more information about the country and its culture on its **Republic of Turkey** Web site.

EDITOR'S CHOICE

The southern slopes face the Anatolian Plateau and are bare of trees. But dense woods of trees and evergreens cover the northern slopes.

During summers, dust storms often blow a fine, yellow powder across the plateau. In April and May, locusts sometimes destroy the plants in the eastern area.

Eastern Turkey has mild summers. However, the mountains have very cold winters. Temperatures dip as low as –40°F.

The majority of the Anatolian Plateau is dry throughout the year. Cold winters and snowstorms blanket the Central Anatolian Plateau.

Southwest Turkey has mild, rainy winters. Hot, dry summers often reach temperatures above 90°F.

East Anatolia

The eastern section of the Anatolian Plateau has a severe climate and rugged terrain. This is where the Pontus and Taurus mountains meet. Mount Ararat is located here. Much of the East Anatolia region is remote.

Southeast Anatolia

The Arabian Platform is in Southeast Anatolia. It is south of the Anti-Taurus Mountains in eastern Turkey. The platform has rolling hills and a broad plateau surface. It extends into Syria.

Mediterranean

The Taurus Mountains separate the narrow coastal plains of the Mediterranean region from Anatolia.

Sandy beaches and hot, dry summers make the Mediterranean area ideal for tourists. Winters are mild, yet wet. The annual rainfall varies from 20 to 28 inches along the Mediterranean coast.

Toward the east are plains. Limestone formations here make up collapsed caverns and sinkholes.

Thirty million years ago, Mount Erciyes, a now-extinct volcano on the Central Anatolian Plateau, erupted repeatedly, covering what is now called Cappadocia in volcanic ash. This ash turned to soft rock, which was eroded by both wind and water, leaving behind unique rock formations, including those shown here.

Earthquakes

Turkey is located in one of the world's more active earthquake and volcano regions. The most earthquake-prone part of Turkey is an arch-shaped region. It stretches from Kocaeli to the area north of Lake Van. This lake is on the border of Armenia and Georgia.

In 1840 an earthquake on Mount Ararat shifted volcanic rock southward. It destroyed a village of about two thousand people.

The most severe earthquake of the twentieth century occurred in Erzincan on December 28 and 29, 1939. The earthquake destroyed most of the city. About 160,000 people died.[3]

Chapter 3 ▶

Islam

It is difficult to sleep late in Turkey. As the first dawn light peeks through, a spiritual leader sounds a call to prayer from the minarets: "[Allah] is most great. [Allah] is most great. I testify that there is no god but [Allah]. I testify that Muhammad is the Prophet of [Allah]. Arise and pray; [Allah] is most great. [Allah] is most great. There is no god but [Allah]."[1] The minarets are tall, slender towers that surround the mosque. A mosque is a building where Muslims worship Allah, the Islamic name for God.

More than ninety-nine percent of the people who live in Turkey are Muslim. Muslims practice Islam as their religion. It is estimated that the other 0.2 percent of Turkish citizens are Jews and Christians. In 1995, there were about 20,000 Jews and 140,000 Christians living in Turkey. Most Christians in Turkey are Armenian, Greek, or Syrian Orthodox.

In modern cities, the prerecorded call to prayer is played over loudspeakers in the minaret towers. When Muslims hear the call, they are to

The Sultanahmet Mosque, located in Istanbul, was built by Sultan Ahmet I from 1609 to 1616. It is also known as the Blue Mosque because of the blue tiles used to decorate the upper level of the building. The Blue Mosque is the only mosque in Turkey to have six minarets.

kneel on their prayer carpets. They are to bow down while facing toward Mecca, Saudi Arabia, and pray to Allah for at least five minutes before beginning their day.

Five times during the day—dawn, mid-day, afternoon, just after sunset, and evening—Muslims are supposed to stop everything they are doing. Each time, they are to pull out their prayer mats, face Mecca, bow to the ground, and pray. On Fridays, it is customary that only Muslim men go to a mosque to pray. At the mosque an Imam reads from the Qur'an, Islam's holy book. An Imam is a political leader and religious guide.

Although its impact varies across the country, Islam is a large part of the Turks' culture and lifestyle.

In the Beginning

"In the beginning . . ." reads the Torah, Bible, and Qur'an. Jewish and Arab people both trace their family lines back to Adam and Eve, through Shem, to Noah, and on to Abraham. However, this is where the Jews and Arabs split. Abraham had two sons. His firstborn, Ishmael, was born of his wife's Egyptian maid, Hagar. His younger son, Isaac, was born to Sarah, Abraham's wife.

The Torah tells a story of how God tested Abraham. God told Abraham to sacrifice Isaac on an altar. But the Qur'an reads that it was Ishmael, not Isaac. Abraham took Ishmael up the mountain to be sacrificed to Allah. On the rest of the account they agree. God sent a ram to be slaughtered in place of the son.

Sarah became jealous of Hagar and Ishmael. She demanded Abraham cast them into the desert. The Qur'an tells how they traveled to Mecca.

The Arabs are from Ishmael's family tree. From Isaac came the Hebrews, who are the ancestors of most Jewish people today.

The Jews continued to worship one God. At some point in history, the Arab people wandered away from their faith in one God. They became polytheistic. They worshiped many gods. By the early seventh century, they worshiped animals and nature.

Muhammad

Muhammad founded Islam. The first biography of Muhammad was not written until about one hundred years after his death. However, Muslim tradition says Muhammad was born in Mecca, a town in Western Arabia (now Saudi Arabia) around A.D. 570. He was orphaned at a young age. He lived with his uncle and took care of his uncle's sheep. As a young man, he married an older widow, Khadija. Muhammad looked after her trading business.

Worshippers gather outside of Sacred Mosque (shown here), located in Mecca, Saudi Arabia. Mecca is the most holy city in Islam.

Angelic Visit

When Muhammad wanted to be alone, he went to a cave on Jabal al-Nour, known as the Mountain of Light. It is a mountain outside of Mecca. During one visit to this cave, the Cave of Hira, in about A.D. 610, an angel appeared to Muhammad. The angel commanded him, "Read." Muhammad was illiterate. He told the angel he could not read. The angel insisted three times that he read. Then the angel taught him a verse.

Muhammad ran home. He told his wife what had happened. One of Khadija's cousins was a Christian monk. He said it must have been the angel Gabriel. The angel must have chosen Muhammad to be a prophet, the priest said. Khadija was the first convert to Islam. Islam means "the peace that comes when one's life is surrendered to God."[2]

Muhammad Preached One God

Muhammad preached Islam to his tribesmen, the Quraish. Instead of being glad to hear there was only one God, they became furious. People traveled a long way to Mecca to worship animals and many gods of nature, including stones. The Quraish merchants had built profitable businesses selling to the people who came to worship idols. If people listened to Muhammad and stopped worshiping idols, then the businessmen would lose money. For this reason, merchants called Muhammad a liar and madman.

The Quraish merchants could not convince Muhammad to stop preaching against worshiping idols. Next, they tried to bribe him. He would not quit preaching. Muhammad's followers heard rumors of plots to kill him.

The Departure

In A.D. 622, Muhammad and his followers left Mecca. They moved to Medina, about two hundred miles across the Arabian Desert. This journey is called the *hijra*. Hijra means "departure." For Muslims this date is the first year of their calendar.

In Medina, Muhammad started the first Muslim community. He set up laws and built the first mosque.

Qur'an

For about twenty-three years, Muhammad heard voices that told him Allah's word. The Qur'an, written around 650, is believed by Muslims to be the direct word of Allah. Qur'an means "recitation" in Arabic. This religious book is four fifths the length of the Christian New Testament. The Qur'an is divided into 114 chapters.

Jihad

In 622, Muhammad wrote the Constitution of Medina. This document allowed Jews and other

Muslims believe that Muhammad was the last prophet, and therefore the Qur'an is superior to any earlier revelations from God.

non-Muslims to travel, trade, and have freedom of thought and expression. When Muhammad thought that someone violated this constitution, he proclaimed a jihad.

Jihad means "to struggle." The Qur'an teaches that a person who is oppressed wrongly can defend himself. A person who engages in jihad is called a *mujahid,* or "struggler for Allah." The Qur'an teaches that if anyone dies in a jihad, he will automatically go to heaven.

Extremist Muslims believe they need to stand up against all opposition on a matter of principle. Even if it means they will die. This is why some believers are willing to be suicide bombers. They believe as a mujahid they are committing jihad against satanic forces of evil.[3]

Pillars of Faith

In Muhammad's last address to the people before he died in 632, he outlined the Five Pillars of Islam.

Pillar Number I:

Faith—All Muslims must declare that there is no God but Allah and that Muhammad is his prophet.

Pillar Number II:

Prayer—Every Muslim should pray five times a day, facing toward Mecca.

Pillar Number III:

Giving of Alms—A Muslim must give 2.5 percent to 10 percent of his capital (money and all he owns) to charity.

Pillar Number IV:

Fasting—One month a year, called "Month of Ramadan," Muslims must not eat, drink, smoke, or take part in sexual intercourse during daylight hours.

Pillar Number V:

Pilgrimage to Mecca—Every Muslim must make a pilgrimage to Mecca at least once in his lifetime. He is excused if ill health, extreme poverty, or other serious problems make it impossible. This trip to

Mecca is called the Hajj. It adds merit for a man to enter paradise after he dies.

Sunnis and Shi'ites

Muhammad united the Arab world, but when he died there was a split among Muslims. The main split was between two groups, the Sunnis and Shi'ites. They disagreed over who should be the first caliph, the spiritual leader of Islam. The Shi'ites insisted it should be Ali, the first male convert and Muhammad's son-in-law. Instead, the Sunnis elected one of Muhammad's fathers-in-law, Abu Bakr, as the first caliph.

Today, about 90 percent of Muslims are Sunni. Ten percent are Shi'ites. Most Shi'ites live in Iran, southern Iraq, and South Asia.[4]

Whirling Dervishes

By the eleventh century A.D. a new sect of Islam emerged from the urban artisan class. They practiced a form of mysticism called Sufism. One Sufi scholar and poet, Jalal ad-Din Rumi, lived in Persia. Rumi moved to Iconium (present-day Konya), Turkey, where he founded a Sufi order that used mysticism, music, and dance in its form of worship.

Men spun and danced in circles until they fell into trances. They were known in the West as Whirling Dervishes. Rumi wrote a six-volume work of spiritual teaching and Sufi lore. This book

The Whirling Dervishes were nicknamed this by Westerners because of the whirling rituals the dervishes performed. These rituals are considered to be an act of love and a show of religious faith. In combination with music and the chanting of poetry, this whirling has been said to create a sense of ecstasy for the faithful.

is sometimes called "the Qur'an in Persian." People even sing the words of his book.

After Turkey became a secular-ruled republic in 1924, the government closed dervish retreats.

Festival of Charity

Ramadan, the Month of Fasting, ends with celebration of Eid ul-Fitr, or the Festival of Charity. After not eating or drinking anything during daylight hours for an entire month, Muslims enjoy this festival filled with favorite foods and drinks. Elders also give money or food to the poor and to children. Everyone eats in homes after prayer at the mosque.

Festival of Sacrifice

Eid al-Adha, or the Festival of Sacrifice, is in honor of Abraham and his willingness to sacrifice

Ishmael. It takes place as the last rite of the annual pilgrimage to Mecca. The day begins with prayer. Then men sacrifice a sheep, cow, or camel. Afterward, the pilgrims eat some of the meat and give the rest to the poor.

Religion in Turkey Today

There are about one billion Muslims in the world today. Turkey is home to the fifth largest Muslim population in the world.[5] However, Turkey is one of the few Muslim countries run by a secular government. Evidence of the country's secular ways include a 1999 ban on women wearing traditional Islamic head scarves in schools, universities, and public offices. Furthermore, in foreign affairs, Turkey has not entered into any international conferences or alliances on the basis of common religion since it became a democracy in 1924. At the same time, however, the Turkish government does play some role in religion. A government agency called the Religious Affairs Directorate controls where mosques are built, pays the salary of most Imams, monitors sermons, and regulates religious schools.

Culture

Turkish culture is a blend of cultures from kingdoms of the East and West. The culture developed over centuries in two ways. People migrated from Asia to Anatolia. And tribes conquered the peninsula.

Languages

About 90 percent of Turkey's citizens speak Turkish.[1] However, an estimated thirty-three other languages are also spoken in the country.[2] These include Kurdish, Arabic, Greek, Armenian, and Ladino. Many of Turkey's Christians still speak Aramaic. This is the language in which much of the New Testament was written. Caucasian languages are also spoken in Turkey.

Of four thousand languages worldwide, Turkish is the sixth or seventh most spoken language. About 120 million people speak Turkish. But only half of those people live in Turkey.

Turkish is an ancient language. In the past, the written language had been based on the Arabic alphabet. It was a difficult language to learn how

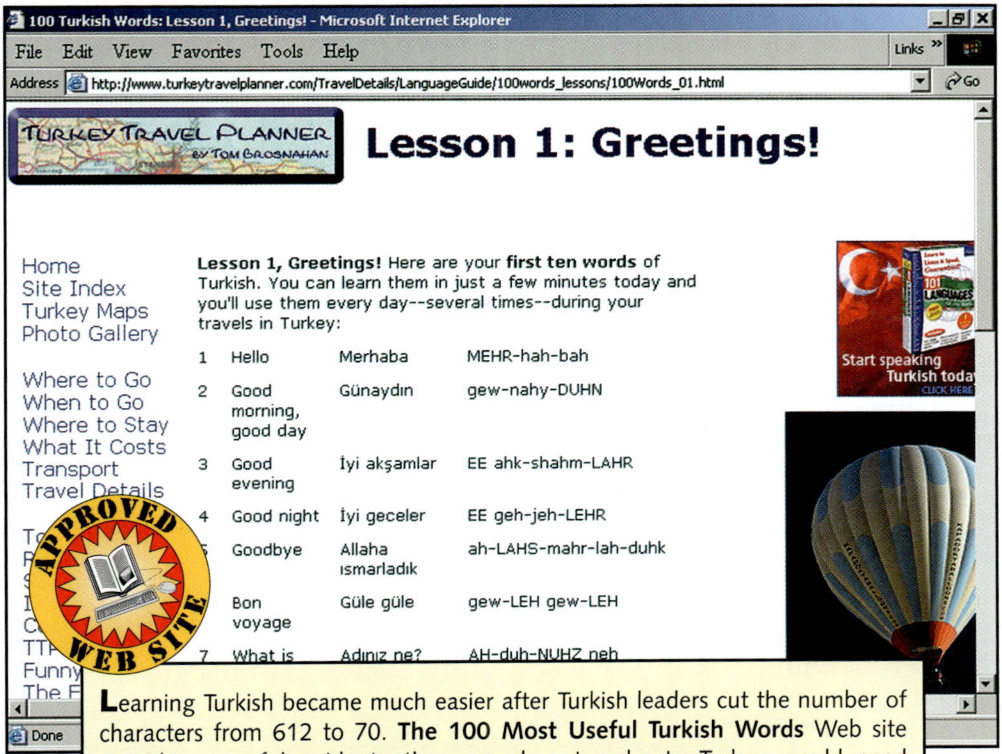

Learning Turkish became much easier after Turkish leaders cut the number of characters from 612 to 70. **The 100 Most Useful Turkish Words** Web site provides a useful guide to those words a traveler to Turkey would need to know.

to read or write. As a result, about 90 percent of the people in Turkey were unable to read.

However, in 1928, Turkish leaders decided to create a new written language based on phonics. In Turkey, Turkish is now written using the Latin alphabet and Arabic numbers. Many European languages, including English, also use the Latin alphabet and Arabic numbers. This decreased the Turkish language from 612 characters to only 70 characters, including numbers, capitals, and signs. Since this change was made, the literacy rate has soared to an estimated 86.5 percent.[3]

Education

Education in Turkey is free. Both boys and girls are required to attend school through eighth grade. After eighth grade, more boys than girls attend higher educational schools. Girls, especially those who live in rural areas, are three times more likely than boys to be illiterate.[4]

Turkey has many professional and technical schools. These are similar to regular and vocational high schools in the United States. Beginning at age twelve, students attend professional and technical schools for up to six years. Once students complete this schooling, they may attend one of the country's fifty-two state universities, twenty-three

Ministry of Culture and Tourism

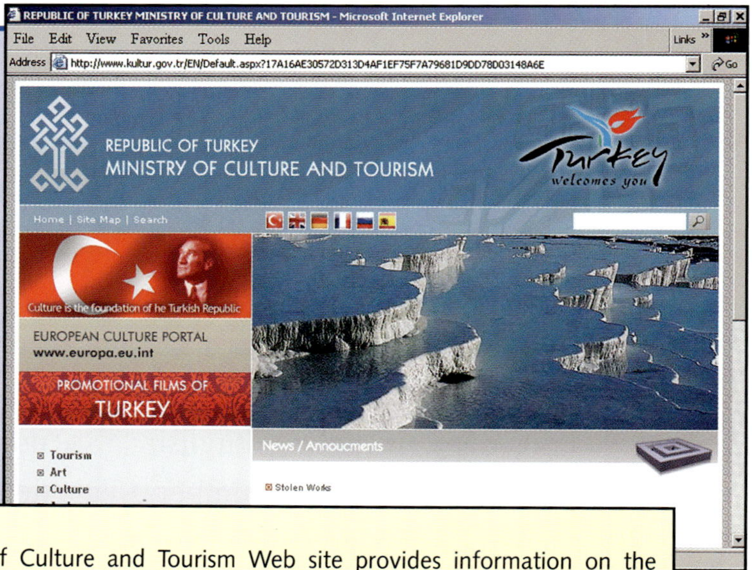

Turkey's Ministry of Culture and Tourism Web site provides information on the country's art, culture, archaeology, history, and more.

EDITOR'S CHOICE

Access this Web site from http://www.myreportlinks.com

private universities, and two higher institutes of technology.

Rural Life

As of 1995, about 35 percent of the population lives in rural areas.[5] Most are either farmers or herders.

The family, with the oldest man as the head, is the most important unit in villages. Extended families work together. They help, protect, and share with their relatives.

Most big landowners live in coastal villages along either the Black Sea or Aegean Sea. Farmers who do not own land work as tenant farmers for the landowners. The landowners get a certain percentage of the tenant farmers' profits.

Villages in southeastern Turkey are mostly Arab and Kurdish. About 12 million to 15 million Kurds live in Turkey. This is about half of all Kurds in the world.[6] The Kurds organize their groups, called tribes, around a common male distant relative who owns a lot of land. In Kurdish tribes, several families may own a lot of land. About half of the families own small plots. And about 10 to 15 percent of the families do not own any land at all. These landless families labor on the farms or tend flocks of sheep or goats for the big landowners. It is common for the Kurdish herders to migrate across many countries' borders.[7]

City and Town Life

In ancient Turkey, nomadic tribes wandered Asia Minor. The first cities in the Anatolian Peninsula formed from caravans. People set up large tents to trade wares, food, and livestock. As they were in ancient times, Turkish cities are the place of merchants and artisans, politicians and military leaders, judges and scholars. Cities are where people go to shop, dine in restaurants, visit theaters, listen to music, and dance at clubs. It is where

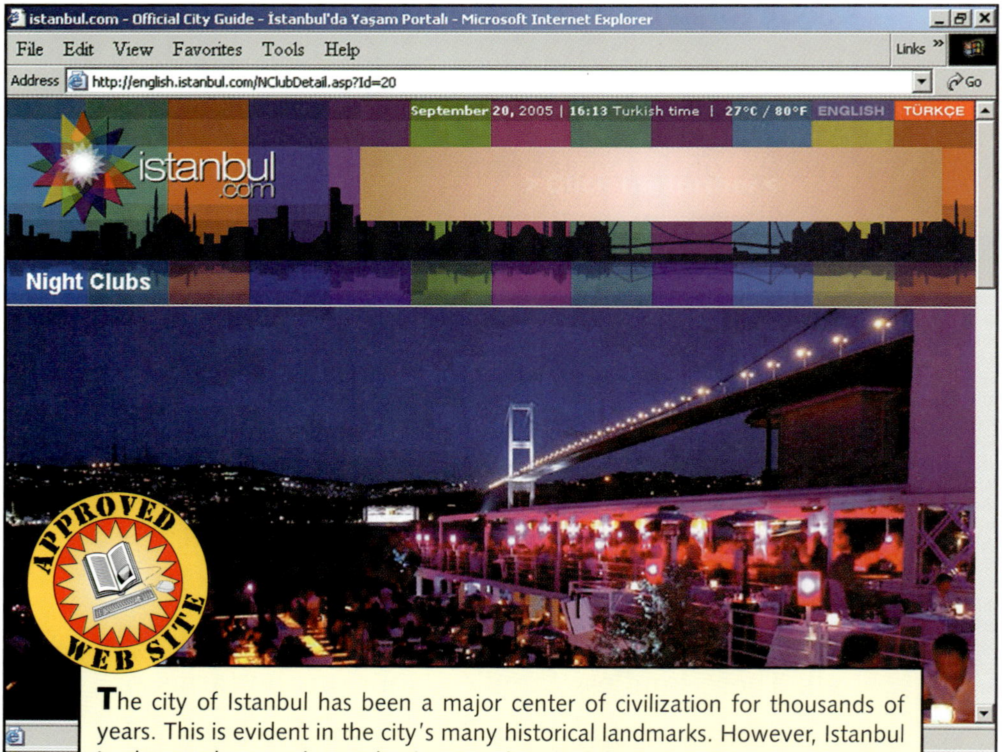

The city of Istanbul has been a major center of civilization for thousands of years. This is evident in the city's many historical landmarks. However, Istanbul is also modern, with trendy shops and nightclubs, such as this one located along the Bosporus. Read more about this city's past and present on the **Explore Istanbul** Web site.

lights are bright and streets can get crowded. It is where the most people gather, work, and live.

If you visit a city today in Turkey, you will find some things very similar to United States cities. For example, American fast-food chains such as McDonald's, Arby's, and Domino's can be found in Istanbul. You can also buy a soda and snacks from 7-Eleven, an American convenience store. However, most shops specialize in foods and goods from Turkey.

Everything from clothing and kitchen utensils to tea and jewelry can be bought at ancient covered bazaars. Be sure to haggle with the shop owner for a bargain! Visitors that miss the malls in the United States can find lots of indoor malls in modern Turkish cities.

Istanbul

For twenty-seven centuries, Istanbul represented the bridge between East and West. It stood as the capital for two great civilizations: the Roman and Byzantine empires. Once called Constantinople, Istanbul is no longer the capital of modern-day Turkey.

Originally a trading center, Istanbul still thrives with shops and malls and bazaars. On the noisy, narrow streets, cars must go slowly around carts pulled by donkeys.

The city is now an international banking and commerce center. Public schools and universities make Istanbul an educational center as well. Members of mosques, churches, and synagogues coexist in this multireligious, multicultural, and multiethnic heart of Turkey.

Ankara, the Capital

When Turkey became a republic in 1923, Mustafa Kemal Pasha decided to move the seat of government away from the country's spiritual center, Istanbul. He chose Ankara, situated on the plain of Central Anatolia.

Like all of Turkey, Ankara is steeped in history. Legend says Amazon women laid the foundation for the first city. While archaeologists have not found evidence of this, they have identified Hittite ruins from 1200 B.C. In addition, Ankara once was the capital for the Galatians. They ruled the area before the Romans.

Today, Ankara is the political and cultural center of modern Turkey. Aside from mosques and universities, you can find museums, nightclubs, and bazaars. Tourists can visit churches carved into volcanic rock as well as underground cities, Roman bathhouses, and a citadel.

Izmir

Izmir is the third largest city in Turkey. About 2 million people live there. It is located on the Gulf of Izmir.

Anitkabir, the mausoleum of Mustafa Kemal Atatürk built in 1944, sits atop a hill overlooking Turkey's capital city of Ankara. Shown here is the dramatic changing of the guard.

Many believe the Greek poet Homer was born in Izmir, then commonly known as Smyrna, around 850 B.C. An important trading port, Izmir has been rocked by wars and earthquakes.

Toward the end of the fifteenth century, Jews driven from Spain settled in Smyrna. By the eighteenth and nineteenth centuries, the city became a big commercial port.

Mustafa Kemal overtook Greek control of Smyrna on September 9, 1922. Shortly after, a fire burned down a wooden house storing weapons. The explosions and fires destroyed the rest of the city. Kemal ordered the city rebuilt. He officially named it Izmir, the Turkish version of Smyrna.

APPROVED WEB SITE

Perry-Castañeda Library Map Collection: Turkey Maps

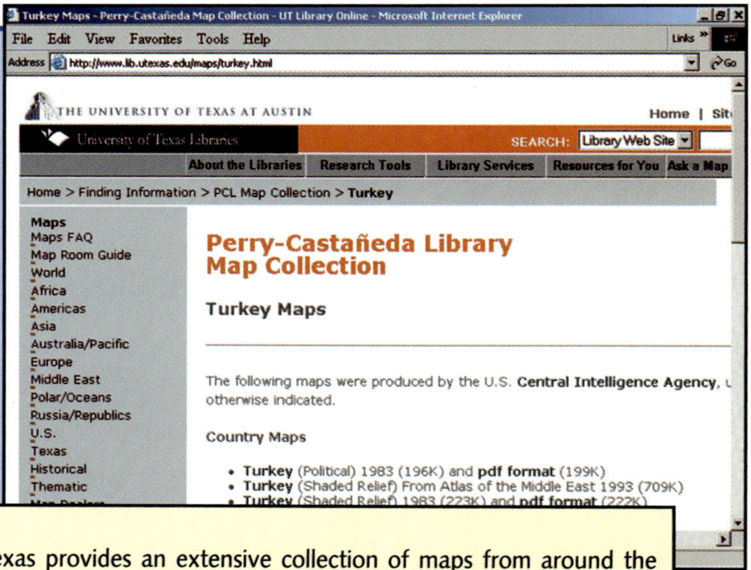

The University of Texas provides an extensive collection of maps from around the world. On this site you can view present-day and historical maps of Turkey.

EDITOR'S CHOICE

Access this Web site from http://www.myreportlinks.com

Today, wide boulevards are lined with office buildings and apartment houses painted in white or soft pastels. The city is an important industrial center. Museums and art galleries attract tourists. In addition, like everywhere else in Turkey, there are still remains of past civilizations for tourists to visit.

Adana

Adana means "city of the bull king." The Hittites settled Adana in about 2000 B.C. It sits in the center of the Cilician plain between two rivers, the Seyhan and the Ceyhan. Adana is the fourth largest Turkish city in population and a commercial and industrial center. Many Arabs and Kurds settled in shanty houses outside the center of town.

Antakya

Antakya spills over both sides of the River Asi. One of Alexander the Great's generals founded the city, naming it Antioch. It was part of a crucial trade route between Asia, the Middle East, and the Mediterranean. By A.D. 64, Antioch ranked as the third most important city in the Roman Empire.

Saint Peter and Saint Paul both lived in Antioch during their lives. Today, Sunday mass is still held in front of Saint Peter's Grotto, a tiny cave high up on a cliff where Peter is believed to have preached.

Earthquakes and war have destroyed much of old Antioch. However, Roman mosaics showing

APPROVED WEB SITE

Historic Figures: Alexander III of Macedon (356–323 B.C.)

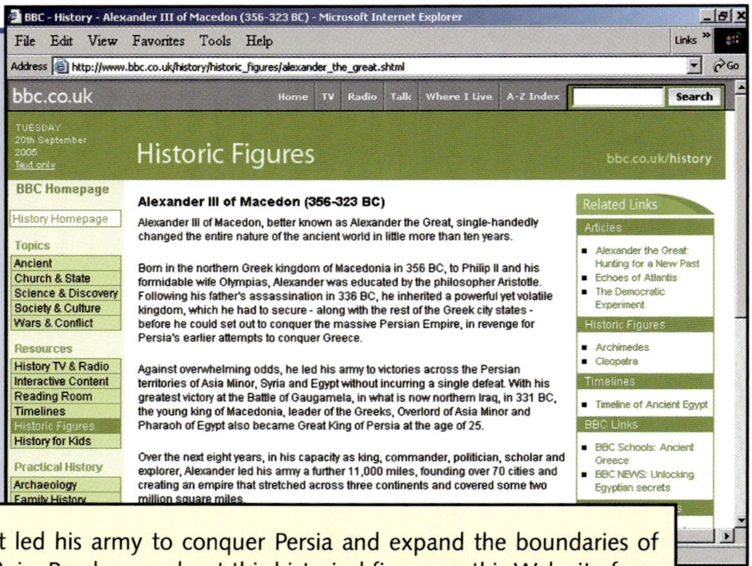

Alexander the Great led his army to conquer Persia and expand the boundaries of ancient Greece into Asia. Read more about this historical figure on this Web site from the BBC.

Access this Web site from http://www.myreportlinks.com

mythology figures survived. The mosaics are kept in a museum.

Citizens of Antakya are mostly bilingual. They speak Arabic and Turkish.

Architecture

One of the seven wonders of the ancient world is located at Ephesus. Around 550 B.C., a Lydian king rebuilt the destroyed Temple of Artemis to worship the goddess of fertility. The new temple was the first huge architectural building made entirely of marble. It burnt to the ground on July 20, 356 B.C. It was rebuilt around 350 B.C. and stood until

A.D. 401. Today, only a bit of the foundations remain.

The Romans built the Aspendos Theater sometime between A.D. 161 and 180. It is similar to the Colosseum in Rome. For entertainment, the Romans pitted gladiators against wild animals in the amphitheater. During the Seljuk period in the thirteenth century, an architect turned the theater into an imperial palace. Today, Aspendos Theater, which seats more than fifteen thousand people, is still used as an amphitheater. Only you will see a ballet or hear an opera rather than the sounds of wild animals and gladiators.

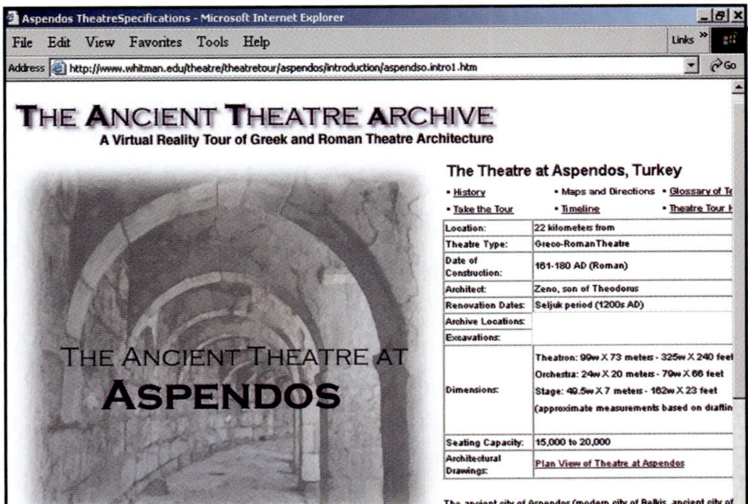

The Ancient Theatre Archive: The Ancient Theatre at Aspendos

The Aspendos Theater is one of the most well-preserved theaters from the Roman Empire period. Whitman College provides information on this theater and a virtual tour.

Access this Web site from http://www.myreportlinks.com

In Istanbul, the cathedral Hagia Sophia was built from A.D. 532 until 537 during the Byzantine era. Its dome is 102 feet wide and 184 feet high. At the end of the fifteenth century the Ottomans converted the church to a mosque. Today it is a museum.

Tiles

For potters and tile makers, the right clay is essential. Artisans found this ideal clay in Western Turkey in Iznik and Kutahya.

According to legend, an angel sent by God to protect Hagia Sophia during its construction appeared before the architect's son. The angel promised to watch over the tools if the boy hurried laborers through their lunch break. When the architect heard about the angel, he did not allow his son to return. The angel was therefore obliged to watch over the church forever.

In the eighth and ninth centuries, Muslim potters learned from Chinese prisoners of war how to make ceramics. These Muslim potters had worked with clays in the Mesopotamian area of Persia. They created tiles to adorn Islamic buildings. Persian potters fled from Mongol invaders in the A.D. 1220s and settled in Iznik, which became a tile and pottery center. Armenian Christians also made tiles and pottery, but they settled in Kutahya. Many of these tiles and pottery vessels were used in Armenian cathedrals.

Carpets

Marco Polo, in the thirteenth century, wrote in his travel log that in Anatolia, ". . . the choicest carpets in the world are made, and those with the loveliest colors." The art of making knotted carpets came to Anatolia during the eleventh century when the Seljuk dynasty conquered Asia Minor. The Seljuks came from Central Asia, where it is believed the art of carpet making originated.

Carpets are made of cotton, wool, or silk. They are used to cover bare floors and make it more comfortable to walk, sit, and kneel, especially during prayer time.

If you turn over a carpet, you will see that the backing is a grid. Carpets are made by crossing horizontal strands with vertical strands of threads. Turkish carpets are made by knotting the rows of

The Turks have long been famous for their beautiful rugs such as the one shown here. The oldest known surviving carpet was found in the grave of a Sycthian prince and dates from the fifth century B.C. It was woven with the Turkish double knot.

threads. The yarn is then cut to produce the "fleece," or pile, of the carpet.

Over time, Turkish rugs evolved to become different from carpets made elsewhere. The Turkish women even designed their own unique knot. Unlike the Persian knot, the Turkish knot is symmetrical. The symmetrical knot is larger and square, and it makes geometric designs. To create decorations, strands of different colors are used to create the knots. Each knot is used much like a tile in a mosaic.

Handicrafts

Women in the Middle East invented knitting. It is possible that Turkish knitting was created by shepherds' wives since the threads and patterns are similar to those of rug weaving. Today, women knit in Turkey's public parks, railroad stations, and buses. However, only in rural villages do older women still knit in the traditional Turkish style. Some people have noted that the art of Turkish knit products is disappearing.[8]

In traditional Turkish knitting, the yarn is tensioned around the neck and flicked with the thumb to make the stitches. Designs are elaborate and colorful.

Musical Instruments

Turkish instruments include the zither, lute, tambura, tambourine, and reed flute. String, woodwind, and percussion instruments are handmade from trees, plants, and the skin, bone, and horns of animals.

A *baglama* is the one instrument that most represents Turkish folk music. A baglama is a stringed instrument similar to a long-necked lute, or small guitar. It originated as a one-stringed, leather-covered lute played by hitting the string. Through the centuries, musicians added strings, until the lute-like instrument developed seven strings and various sizes.

Single or double reed flutes, called a shepherd's pipe, are mostly used in mystic and religious music. Drums beat in cadence to the *zurna*. A zurna is a double reed instrument similar to an oboe. Musicians play drums and zurnas at military marches, weddings, and circumcision festivals.

The Armenian woodwind instrument, the *duduk,* has been played since 1200 B.C. The duduk is a short apricot wood tube with nine finger holes, a thumbhole, and a large double reed into which the player blows.

Traditional Turkish music is monophonic. Monophonic means all the musicians play the same melody.

Soccer

Soccer is a popular sport in Turkey. In Turkey, however, it is called football.

Soccer is so important in the country that during the 2002 World Cup tournament, business meetings, office hours, schools, and even the prime minister's press conference were arranged according to soccer match times. Everyone wanted to watch the games on television.

Turkey's national football team placed third in the 2002 World Cup. The team placed third in the 2003 Confederations Cup.

Horse Sports

Horses were very important to the ancient Turks. To sharpen their cavalry skills for war, the Turks played a game called *jereed.*

Jereed is still played in parts of Turkey today. To play jereed, horsemen line up across from each other. Two teams of horsemen stand in rows of six, eight, or twelve players. Each player holds a long

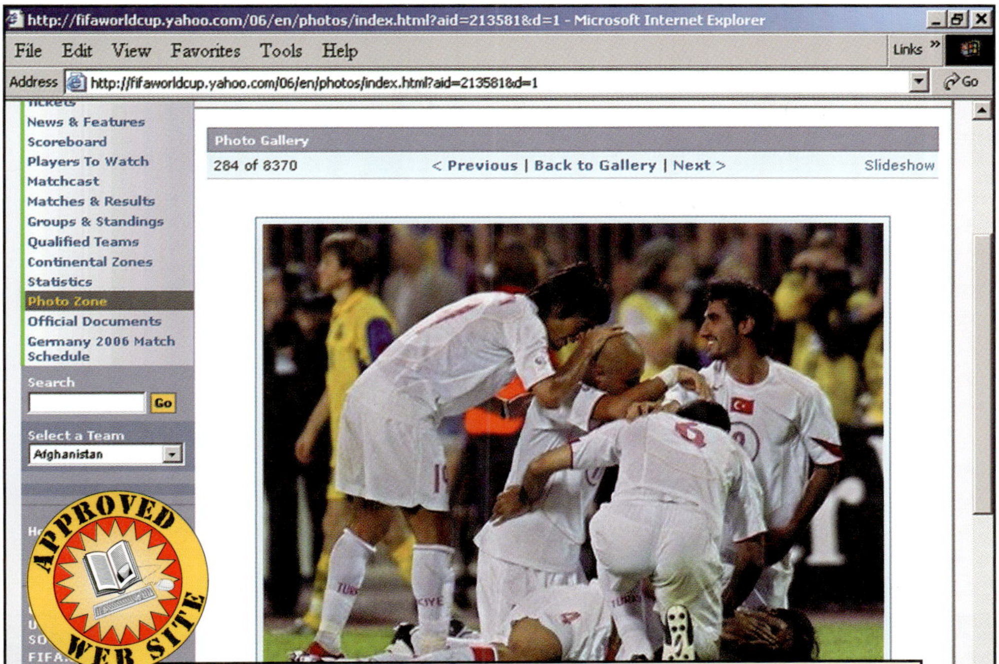

The Turkish soccer team celebrates after winning a 2006 World Cup qualifying match against the Ukrainian national team. On the **FIFA World Cup: Germany 2006: Turkey** Web site, read about Turkey's soccer team and follow its progress leading up to the 2006 World Cup.

stick with a blunt end made of poplar wood. The object is to throw a stick at the opposing player and hit him. If someone gets hit, the team scores a point. If a horse gets hit instead, the team loses a point. Even though players wear protective gear, sometimes they are permanently hurt or even killed. Referees decide who wins the game of jereed.

Oil Wrestling

For more than six centuries, in early July, an oil wrestling festival takes place at Edirne. Wrestlers wear breeches made of cow or goat leather. They oil their entire bodies with olive oil before bouts. Musicians play drums and zurnas as the men wrestle. The wrestling matches go on for three days. On the last day, the two wrestlers who have won the most matches compete for the Gold Belt, made with real gold.

Backgammon

For a game of wits instead of strength, many people in Turkey play backgammon. Backgammon is a game of chance and skill played by two people

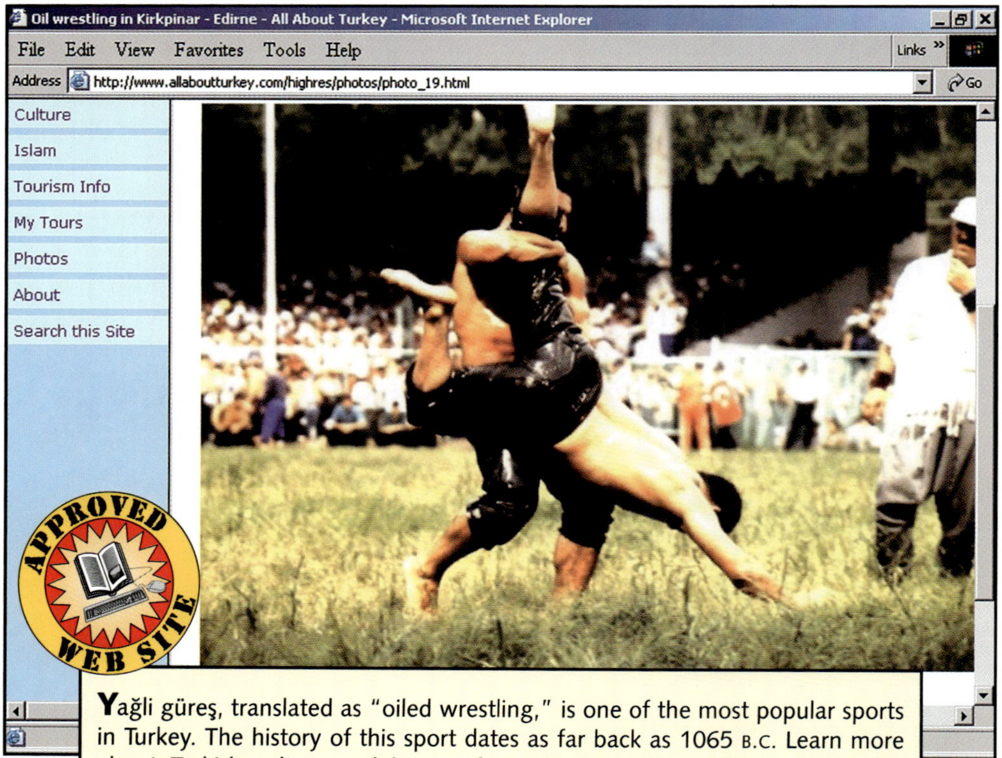

Yağli güreş, translated as "oiled wrestling," is one of the most popular sports in Turkey. The history of this sport dates as far back as 1065 B.C. Learn more about Turkish culture and history from the same Web site as **All About Turkey: Islam.**

on a specially marked board, and it is one of the oldest known games in history. Backgammon was first played in the Persian Empire. Originally, the game was played on a wooden board, using stones as markers, and dice made from bones, stones, wood, or pottery.[9]

Today it is common to see men sitting outside Turkish coffeehouses playing backgammon.

Cuisine

Turkish food includes all cultures that most influenced the Turks in their migration from Asia to the Anatolian peninsula. The Turks borrowed dishes such as dumplings, vegetable stews, kebabs, and rice and flavored them to become their own.

But they also added their own foods and ways of preparing them. It is guessed that the Turks stuffed pasta and intestines and vegetables before the Chinese did. The most well-known food eaten, and named, by the Turks is yogurt, made from fermented milk. They even make yogurt soup.

Turks eat three meals a day. A typical breakfast consists of soft-boiled eggs, cheese, olives, and jam and butter on fresh-baked bread. They drink tea. In the winter, sausage or beef may be added to their breakfast. Lunch is a hot meal. Dinner is the main meal of the day when the entire family gathers together at the kitchen table. Dinner usually begins with soup. Meat, chicken, or fish, and

Men first began to play backgammon in coffeehouses during the Ottoman Period.

a vegetable or beans is served next. In the summer, Turks eat salads, and in the winter, pickles. After the main meal is served, side dishes made with olive oil are added to the table. Finally, they eat dessert, such as melon and other fresh fruit, milk pudding, or fruit compotes.

Chapter 5 ▶

Ancient Peoples

From the snowcapped Taurus Mountains spring the Tigris and Euphrates rivers. These rivers flow down onto the plains of modern-day Iraq. This area forms what is known as the Fertile

This gold figurine was made sometime between 1400 and 1200 B.C. by the Hittites. Its horned headdress identifies the figurine as a god, and the weapon it holds may suggest that this was meant to be the god of hunting. View other artifacts from various time periods in Turkey's history at **The British Museum: COMPASS Collections Online** Web site.

Crescent. It is believed that all of civilization began in that part of the world.

If you were to visit Turkey, you would literally walk on top of layers and layers of cities. In the Konya Basin, archaeologists uncovered what may have been the world's first urban settlement from about 6500 B.C.[1] Either armies or earthquakes demolished the cities. New invaders built cities on top of the rubble.

Early People of Turkey

Before recorded history, tribes of people, usually related, banded together for common economic purposes and protection. Archaeologists have dug up tombs from the Bronze Age. Statues found show that these primitive people possibly worshiped many gods. Archaeologists discovered iron weapons, clay pots, and cloth made by these early people. But since they did not write, much of their history is lost.

During the early Bronze Age, about 3000 B.C., Assyrian merchants wrote the earliest documents in Anatolia. Business papers, such as bills of sale, prove Anatolia was an active trading center for merchant caravans. The universal language then was Babylonian. "Royal mail" was even sent by messengers.[2]

Archaeologists discovered ore and furnace sites dating from 1500 B.C. It is believed that Southern Anatolia was the center of iron production.[3]

Turkey has such a vast and varied landscape. A variety of peoples occupied it at the same time.

Greeks, 2600–800 B.C.

The Aegean coast of Anatolia was part of the Minoan-Mycenean civilization. During 1050–800 B.C., Greek refugees fled across the sea to Anatolia. It was during the eighth century that Greeks expanded their cities along the coast and founded Byzantium.

Kurds, 2000 B.C.

The Kurds were once goatherders and sheepherders living as nomadic tribes. Nomads wander about to different regions. The Kurds migrated from the Eurasian steppes in about 2000 B.C. to the Taurus Mountains. They settled with other tribes that already lived in the region.[4]

Hittite Empire, 1600–1200 B.C.

Much is known about the Hittites once they settled in Anatolia. This is because they recorded their history. They were the first in Anatolia to do so. Archaeologists unearthed about ten thousand clay tablets. The tablets were discovered in the ruins of the Hittite capital, Hattusas, which is now named Boğzköy.

The Hittites adopted the pagan gods of the native Hatti tribes. It is even believed they took the name *Hittites* from Hatti. The Hittites gave

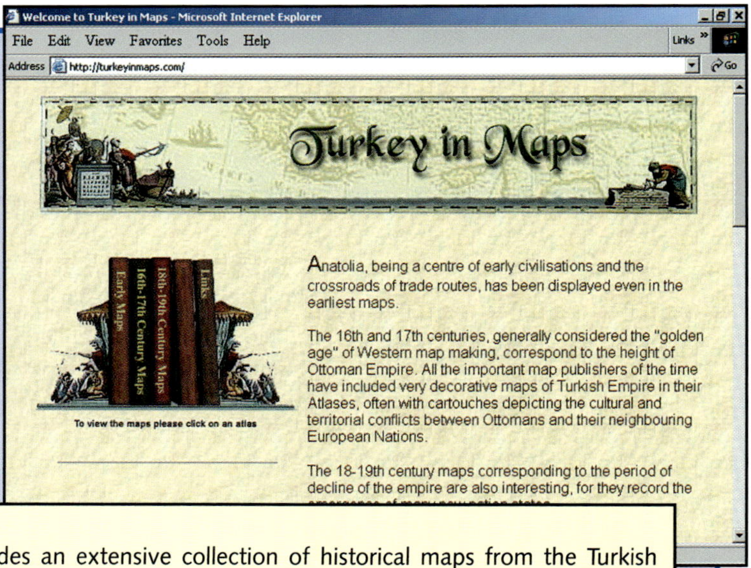

Turkey in Maps

This Web site provides an extensive collection of historical maps from the Turkish region, dating back to 6200 B.C.

Access this Web site from http://www.myreportlinks.com

up their Indo-European language. They switched to the written language, cuneiform alphabet, and literary style of the Semitic cultures of Mesopotamia. However, the Hittites did not change all aspects of their society. They kept their political and social organizations. Local peasants were forced to pay the Hittite warriors rent, for services, and taxes.

Hittites became known for their skills in trading and making agreements with other peoples. In fact, a Hittite ruler signed, in 1269 B.C., what is believed to be one of the earliest peace treaties. The Hittites made peace with the Egyptians. The

Hittite Empire extended from Anatolia through Syria and Mesopotamia.

Phrygians, 1200–695 B.C.

From the twelfth to ninth centuries B.C., there were many uprisings against the kingdoms in Anatolia, including the Hittites. The Phrygians, who were clients of Hittite merchants, rebelled and burned Hattusas in 1200 B.C. Afterward the Hittite state collapsed. The Phrygians ruled most of western and central Anatolia in the ninth century B.C. Their capital was located at Gordium,

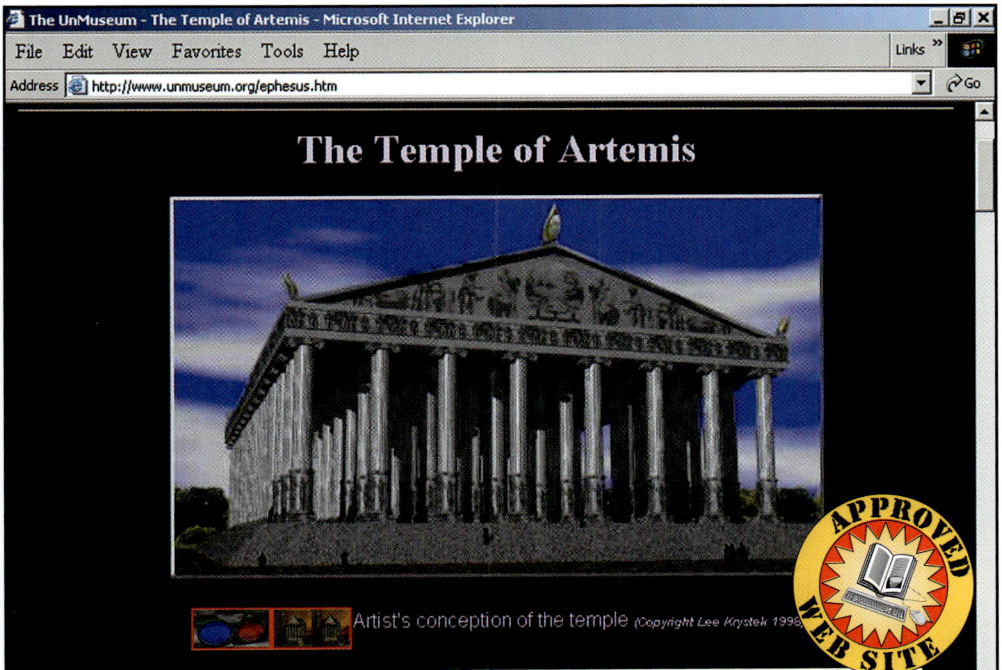

The Temple of Artemis at Ephesus once stood in what is now southeastern Turkey. Although it was rebuilt many times, the Greeks, in 550 B.C., built the temple that is considered to be an ancient wonder of the world. It was burned down in 356 B.C. Learn more about the Temple of Artemis at **The UnMuseum: Temple of Artemis** Web site.

an ancient city near present-day Ankara. The Phrygian civilization disappeared when it was invaded by a nomadic people called the Cimmerians in the seventh century B.C.

Different invaders also invaded other areas of present-day Turkey after the fall of the Hittites. These invaders arrived by both sea and land.

Armenians, 700 B.C.

The Cimmerians also chased the Armenians from the Armenian Plateau in the seventh century B.C. The Armenians fled as refugees to the Lake Van area. At that time, this area was under Persian rule. By 100 B.C., an Armenian kingdom stretched from the Black Sea to the Caspian Sea. However, by then it was under Roman protection. The kingdom acted as a buffer between the Roman and Persian empires.

Persian Empire, 513–334 B.C.

In 546 B.C., King Cyrus Achaemenid of Persia conquered the Lydian kingdom, which included Anatolia. The Persian kingdom ran from the Aegean Sea to the Indus Valley in present-day Pakistan. Persian governors ruled over different regions. But local people conducted daily affairs in cities. As a result, the people of Anatolia adopted Persian manners, dress, arts, and religion.

However, Greeks along the coast resented Persian rule. They did not like how the Persian culture was so different from their own. In 499–494 B.C., Greeks from the Aegean area rebelled against the Persians.

Alexander the Great, 334–323 B.C.

Greek officials in Thrace and Anatolia asked a foreign king to liberate their cities from the Persians. At age twenty-one, Alexander the Great, a Macedonian king and general, marched his troops to Thrace. He crossed the sea to Anatolia. It took four more years to liberate the Greek cities planted in Asia Minor. Eventually, Alexander expanded his empire from the Nile River to the Indus Valley. Greek cities thrived under his rule. When Alexander died eight years after becoming king, his empire was divided among three of his generals.

Alexander the Great was one of history's most successful military commanders.

Roman and Byzantine Empires, 63 B.C.–A.D. 1701

The Roman Empire was the next great power to rise up from the West and spread to the East. By A.D. 116, the Roman Empire had reached its greatest size.

In A.D. 330, Emperor Constantine moved his capital from Rome to Byzantium. The city was renamed Constantinople in honor of the emperor. Constantinople remained the Roman Empire's capital for twelve centuries. In Asia, the Roman Empire was called the Byzantine Empire in reference to the former name of Constantinople.

In A.D. 395, when Emperor Theodosius I died, the kingdom was divided between his two sons. One son ruled the Roman Empire, all lands west of Constantinople. The other son, Arcadius, ruled the Byzantine Empire, which included all lands east of Constantinople. Anatolia was the most productive part of the Roman Empire, which included Greece, Italy, the Balkans, North Africa, and Morocco.[5]

Paul the Apostle introduced Christianity to Anatolia. His early missionary journeys in Turkey were to Antioch, Ephesus, Iconium, Derbe, and Lystra. By A.D. 313, the majority of citizens in Anatolia were Christians. Christianity's influence became not only religious, but also political and economic.

History of the Turks

Turks are believed to be related to the Huns. They settled in Northwest China and Central Asia, including Mongolia. In the sixth or seventh century, the Turks migrated west. One clan, called Oguz Turks, embraced Islam in the tenth century. Descendants of the Oguz Turkish clan leader, Seljuk, moved to Persia (Iran and Iraq). They worked for the Islamic religious leaders in

When the Roman emperor Constantine moved his empire's capital to Byzantium, the city was renamed Constantinople in his honor. In 1453, the city's name was changed yet again to Istanbul, which it remains today. However, the name was not officially changed until March 28, 1930.

Baghdad. The religious leaders also held the political power.

Some Turkish horsemen worked as hired warriors, called gazis. Others were slave-soldiers. The gazis were hired to guard borders, collect taxes, and patrol trade routes. But they often raided Byzantine villages to steal from the people.

One Seljuk military leader forced an Islamic spiritual leader to make him a sultan in Persia and Mesopotamia. A sultan held more power than a king. Sultans ruled in political, military, judicial, social, and religious capacities. In theory, a sultan was responsible only to Allah and Allah's law.

Seljuk Empire, A.D. 1071–1243

This Seljuk sultan's successor was Alp Arslan, meaning "The Lion Hero." In A.D. 1071, Alp Arslan led Turkish gazis to Manzikert near Lake Van. There they defeated the Byzantine Army. This opened all of Anatolia for the Turks to conquer.

In 1045, Armenia had been added to the Byzantine Empire. The Armenians were Christians, but they did not unify with the Greek Orthodox Christians. As a result, they did not cooperate together to fight against the Turkish invasion. By the late eleventh century, the Seljuks captured all of Armenia. The Armenians scattered throughout the Byzantine Empire. A great many of them settled in Constantinople.

By 1171, Seljuks won control of most of Anatolia. They replaced the Byzantine officials with Turkish and Muslim leaders. People converted to Islam. The Turkish language and customs took root in the countryside.[6]

The Crusades

The Turks spread Islam throughout the Middle East, across Northern Africa, and into Spain. Leaders of Christian empires in Europe became outraged. On October 27, 1095, Pope Urban II called on knights in France to free Christians under Islamic rule. The pope also wanted to take back Jerusalem from Muslims. This began a series of military campaigns known as the Crusades.[7]

In 1190, during the Third Crusade (1189–92), European soldiers defeated Turks in Asia Minor. Within a few years of holy war, the western third of Anatolia once again came under Byzantine rule.

The Turks fought back. They experienced some successes in the 1190s. However, during the Fourth Crusade (1202–04), in March 1204, French soldiers sacked and torched Constantinople. They killed thousands of Greeks.

The land was divided into different kingdoms. A French count ruled over Constantinople. Independent Greek kingdoms were set up at

Nicaea, (present-day) Trabzon, and Epirus. Turks united with Greeks in Anatolia against Crusaders and invading Mongols.

By the 1330s, Mongol influence disappeared. The gazis fought among themselves for power and land. With war and confusion everywhere in the Middle East, a new power emerged in Anatolia—the Ottoman Turks.

Ottoman Empire, Except For Constantinople, A.D. 1326–1453

The Oguz Turks served the sultan of Rum (Rome) as gazis. The Oguz leader, Estugrul, was given land in northwestern Anatolia. His son, Osman, became the founder of the Osmanli Dynasty. In

The Ottomans

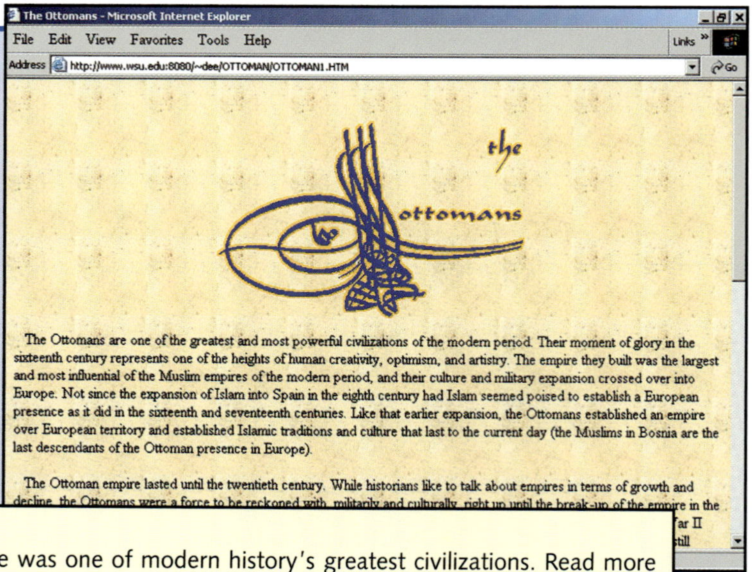

The Ottoman Empire was one of modern history's greatest civilizations. Read more about this empire at this Web site.

Access this Web site from http://www.myreportlinks.com

Europe they called them the Ottomans. Thirty-six sultans from the Ottoman family ruled for six centuries.

Gazis from other territories joined Osman's gazis to raid more areas. Soon Osman's territory expanded into an empire. He declared himself a sultan and organized a central government. In 1323, the last year of Osman's reign, his gazis captured Bursa.

After Osman died, the Ottoman gazis crossed the Dardanelles and set up a European base. They added Thrace, circled Constantinople, and moved the Ottoman government to Edirne. The gazis then invaded Europe. They defeated the Serbs in Kosovo and then conquered the Balkans and then Hungary.

Mongols Invade Anatolia

Meanwhile, the Mongol leader Timur (Tamerlane) invaded the Ottoman Empire in Anatolia. Ironically, many of Timur's cavalrymen used to be Turkish gazis. Timur crushed the Ottoman Army near Ankara in 1402. He captured the Ottoman sultan. The sultan died while held prisoner. For a decade the sultan's four heirs competed for control of what was left of the Ottoman Empire in Anatolia.

By 1420, Ottoman power increased enough to invade Greece. At this time, all that was left of the

Byzantine Empire were a few outposts in Greece and Constantinople. The city had survived as the Byzantine capital by making truces with the Turks. However, although the Ottomans occupied the land passages, the Venetians controlled the seas. Since Constantinople was isolated, supplies were sailed in by Venetian traders.

Constantinople Falls

Mehmet II became the Ottoman sultan in 1444. He soon set out to conquer Constantinople. In 1453, the Ottoman gazis battered Constantinople for fifty days. Soon after sunrise on May 29, 1453, the Ottoman Turks broke through a small gate in the city walls. By sunset, Mehmet II's troops

APPROVED WEB SITE

The World Factbook: Turkey

The Central Intelligence Agency provides information on Turkey's political background, geography, people, economy, government, and more at its Web site.

Access this Web site from http://www.myreportlinks.com

fought to victory. After more than eleven hundred years, the Byzantine capital fell into Muslim hands.

Sultan Mehmet II knew what his victory meant as a religious symbol. Late that Tuesday afternoon, he rode his gray horse to Hagia Sophia. As his first order of business, Mehmet II converted the Greek Orthodox Church into an Islamic mosque.

The sultan made Constantinople his royal capital. He rebuilt the city. Constantinople became known as Istanbul, which means "to the city" in Greek. It replaced Baghdad as the center of Sunni Islam. Mehmet II allowed the Greek Orthodox Church to keep its headquarters in Istanbul, but under his control. He handpicked a monk to lead the Christian church.

Selim I and Süleyman the Magnificent

During Selim I's reign (1512–20), the Ottoman Empire extended southward to include Syria, Palestine, and Egypt. He became protector of the Muslim holy cities Mecca and Medina.

From 1520 to 1566, Selim I's son, Süleyman, ruled. Muslims called him "the lawgiver." In Europe, however, he was known as Süleyman the Magnificent because of all the lands he conquered. When he died in 1566, the Ottoman Empire was a world power. The crescent flag flew over Mecca, Medina, Jerusalem, Damascus,

Süleyman the Magnificent is buried in this Istanbul mausoleum located within Süleymaniye Mosque complex. In addition to being a sultan and military leader, Süleyman was a poet, and during his reign, architecture, art, and literature flourished.

Cairo, Tunis, and Baghdad. The empire extended from Anatolia, to the Balkans, Syria, Palestine, Mesopotamia, Egypt, North Africa, Arabia, and north to the Caucasus, plus a number of other European states.

Decline of the Ottoman Empire

One mistake the Ottoman officials made, though, was to become dependent on European imported goods. The unbalanced trade destroyed native craft industries. The Ottoman Empire became indebted to European nations. This was responsible in part for an economic decline of the Ottoman Empire by the last thirty years of the sixteenth century. There were two other causes of decline: officials competed for leadership within the empire and constant fighting against other nations. In 1571, the Spanish and Portuguese navies defeated the Turkish fleet. Still, the

Ottomans held ground on most fronts. During a forty-seven-year stable period from 1656 to 1703, the gazis invaded Crete and part of the Ukraine and Austria. After the Turks attacked Vienna twice, several nations joined together to fight back. The pope called on armies from Austria, Poland, and Venice, Italy, to fight the Muslims in a holy war. Russia joined the three nations, called the Holy League. Together they drove the Ottomans south of the Danube River and east of the Carpathian Mountains. For the first time ever, the Ottomans admitted defeat. Under terms of treaties in 1699 and 1700, they gave lands back to Austria, Poland, and Russia.

"The Sick Man of Europe"

During the eighteenth century, the Ottoman Empire was continually at war with enemies Persia, Poland, Austria, and Russia. By 1853, the tsar of Russia described the Ottoman Empire as "the sick man of Europe." The "European Question" was how to break up the Ottoman Empire so no one country would gain too much land and therefore too much power.

While battles and land were being lost, other changes also occurred within the empire. A group called the Young Ottoman Movement wanted the empire to be accepted as an equal by European powers. They desired to adopt Western political

Background Note: Turkey

A variety of information on Turkey can be found on this U.S. State Department Web site. Politics and the economy are the two main focal points.

Access this Web site from http://www.myreportlinks.com

systems. The Young Ottomans wished for a central government, an elected parliament, and a written constitution. They called for a secular government where non-Muslims could vote and hold office. One leader of the movement was Midhat Pasha.

It was in this political climate of 1876 that the sultan was overthrown. A new sultan candidate, Abdul Hamid II, seemed sympathetic to the Young Ottomans' cause. In December 1876, Abdul Hamid II approved a constitution written by Midhat Pasha based on European models. It provided for a representative parliament, gave religious liberty, and expanded freedom of expression. However, soon after the new sultan took the throne, he sent Midhat into exile. The sultan called to order the first parliament, but did away with it within a year.

It appeared that political change failed to take root. However, the Young Ottomans reappeared in the early twentieth century as the Young Turks. This time, it would change every branch of Turkish society.

Twentieth-Century Turkey

A group of Turkish Army officers organized the Young Turks, a secret society set on change. In 1907, the Young Turks joined the Committee of Union and Progress (CUP). Its goals were to restore the 1876 constitution and unify the nation. It also wanted a central government run by a parliament.[1]

Revolutions

In July 1908, Turkish Army units in Macedonia rebelled. They called for a constitutional government. Abdul Hamid II said they could elect a parliament in November of that year. CUP won all but one seat.

However, once in power, the Young Turk's government proved unstable. Government officials disagreed as to how changes should be made. In the communities, traditional Muslims and non-Turkish peoples argued about how much control the government should have over citizens. Abdul Hamid II was forced to step down from his position as sultan. His brother, Mehmet V, followed him in office in 1909.

Turkish Odyssey: History

This Web site provides a good overview of the history of the area we now know as Turkey. Find information ranging from the appearance of the Neanderthal man to recent history.

Access this Web site from http://www.myreportlinks.com

Meanwhile, other countries took advantage of the confusion within the Ottoman government. Right after the 1908 revolution, Austria took over Bosnia and Herzegovina. Bulgaria declared independence. Italy started a war in 1911 by claiming Libya. Greece, Serbia, Montenegro, and Bulgaria joined together and invaded Macedonia and Thrace in October 1912. The Ottoman military lost. As a result, the Ottoman Empire lost all of its European lands except the part of eastern Thrace where Istanbul stands.

These land losses led to a military rebellion within the Ottoman Empire. Some members of the Young Turks overthrew the government in

January 1913. This new government only obeyed the constitution for a short time. CUP leaders ruled the empire. The three main leaders were Mehmet Talat Pasha, Ahmet Cemal Pasha, and Enver Pasha, as minister of war.

German Support of Ottomans

During all of the confusion and land losses in the twentieth century, Germany was the only European country to support the Ottoman Empire. Germany invested in the Ottoman economy, and German officers held training and command posts in the Ottoman Army.

As Europe grew closer to war in 1914, Enver wanted to side with Germany. Talat and Cemal proposed to stay neutral. On August 2, 1914, Enver Pasha secretly signed a treaty to support Germany.[2]

World War I

Between November 5 and 6, Russia, Britain, and France declared war on the Ottoman Empire. Within six months, the Ottoman Army of about eight hundred thousand men fought battles on four fronts.[3]

Armenians Killed

During the winter of 1914–15, the Russian Army drove the Ottomans back from the Caucasus Mountains to Lake Van. Armenians in this area

Lake Van is the largest lake in Turkey, covering an area of just under 1.5 square miles. Shown here is Lake Van in the foreground, and in the background is the Church of the Holy Cross, built in A.D. 921 by the Armenians, on Akdamar Island.

viewed Russians as freeing them from the Ottomans. Many Armenians helped the Russian Army.

Enver blamed the Armenians for this setback. He claimed they would rebel from Ottoman rule. He ordered 2 million Armenians to be deported from the war zone by Lake Van. Instead, ethnic Turks and Kurds murdered Armenians in their villages as they fled. It is estimated that somewhere between six hundred thousand to one million Armenians died. Those who survived marched into Syria or escaped behind Russian lines.[4]

Turkey Carved Up

The World War I defeat of Germany and its allies was the final blow to the Ottoman Empire. The countries that won World War I were not forgiving to the Ottoman Empire.

On August 10, 1920, Mehmet VI was forced to sign the Treaty of Sèvres. The Ottomans lost almost all territory in Europe and Asia. According to the treaty, the Ottoman Empire was only supposed to be allowed to keep small parts of Anatolia not claimed by the Greeks, Italians, and French.

Enver, Talat, and Cemal fled to Germany. In 1921, Armenian men murdered Talat and Cemal. The next year, Enver died fighting Russians. During the course of World War I, about 325,000 Ottoman soldiers died and more than 2 million civilians, both Turks and Armenians, were killed.[5]

Nationalist Movement

Mustafa Kemal Pasha, who was later granted the last name of Atatürk by the Grand National Assembly, recruited an army of farmers in the Anatolia countryside. His goal was to resist efforts to tear apart what was left of the Ottoman Empire.

In July and September 1919, Atatürk called together a national congress to form an independent Turkish state. Many of the men at the meeting voted for a Turkish state. They wanted to keep the sultan and caliph as rulers.

The congress and Ottoman officials could not agree on what type of government to set up. Meanwhile, foreign armies occupied Istanbul, Anatolia, and other Ottoman lands. In April 1920, against the will of the Ottoman government, the

In 1934, the national parliament gave Mustafa Kemal the surname Atatürk, meaning "Father of the Turks." Atatürk attained many great achievements in the fifteen years he led Turkey, all of which were in accordance with his motto "Peace at Home, Peace in the World." Learn more about the founder of modern Turkey at the **Mustafa Kemal Atatürk: 1881–1938** Web site.

congress met in Ankara. They elected Atatürk to the presidency. The men adopted laws to organize the new Turkish government.

War of Independence

In 1919, Greek soldiers occupied Edirne, Bursa, and Izmir. The next year, Atatürk fought against the Greeks on Turkish soil. Neither side won. The following year the Turkish Army gained some victories over the Greeks. In July 1920, Atatürk led forces outside of Ankara that defeated the Greek Army in a twenty-day battle.

As a result of the Turks' military successes, the French and Italian militaries pulled out of Anatolia by October 21. Russia was the first European power to sign a treaty recognizing Turkey's new government.

The Turks defeated the Greek Army in August and September 1922 at Izmir. The next step was for the Turks to drive the Greeks out of eastern Thrace, where Istanbul is located. The British proposed a truce. Atatürk accepted. Greek troops withdrew beyond the Maritsa River. However, the troops of those countries that won World War I continued to guard the straits and Istanbul.

Birth of Turkey

In November 1922, the Grand National Assembly, with Atatürk at the head, did away with the sultan position. Sultan Mehmet VI was sent away to Malta. The assembly also did away with the Ottoman government.

Atatürk and representatives of the Turkish government met with the officials from countries that won World War I. They all signed the Treaty of Lausanne setting the boundaries that Turkey has today. The League of Nations gained control of the straits. Turkey assumed 40 percent of the Ottoman debt. Muslim and non-Muslim Turkish people were to be treated equally. Turkey and Greece exchanged ethnic Greek and Turkish citizens. Only

Greeks in Istanbul and Turks in western Thrace and the Dodecanese Islands did not have to move.

On October 29, 1923, the Republic of Turkey was born. The Grand National Assembly named Atatürk president. They decided on Ankara as Turkey's capital.

Atatürk's Reforms

"The civilized world is far ahead of us," Atatürk said when he first took office. "We have no choice but to catch up."[6] He looked toward the West for a model of government and society even though Western culture, customs, and government were the most foreign to heartland farmers and herders in the mountains.

APPROVED WEB SITE

Ministry of Foreign Affairs: Diplomatic Archives: Turkish Presidents

Turkey's Ministry of Foreign Affairs Web site contains information on the lives and political achievements of all the presidents in the country's history. Read about the current president of Turkey, Ahmet Necdet Sezer.

Access this Web site from http://www.myreportlinks.com

Over the next dozen years, Mustafa Kemal Atatürk made sweeping changes at every level of society. First he and the assembly did away with the caliphate. They wished to prove Turkey's government would be secular, not religious. Then the assembly closed religious schools and Whirling Dervish brotherhoods. In 1928, a change was made to the 1924 constitution so that Islam was no longer the official religion of Turkey.

Hat Act

One change that outraged traditionalist citizens was in 1925 when Atatürk outlawed the fez. A fez is a red or purple felt cylinder-shaped hat with a black tassel. Men protested the Hat Act. In response, Atatürk had several dozen protesters sentenced to death, imprisonment, or banishment. That put an end to the Hat Revolution. Men took off their fezzes and adopted Western hats and dress.

The fez hat originated in the city of Fez, Morocco, in northern Africa. It became popular among modernist Ottomans as a replacement for the turban.

The women of Turkey have more rights than women in most other Middle Eastern countries.

Women Gain Liberties

Atatürk also greatly increased freedoms for Muslim women in Turkey. The assembly passed a law in 1926 that allowed civil marriages. The law made it harder for men to divorce their wives. Men were no longer allowed to marry more than one woman.

By 1934, women gained the right to vote and hold office. Tansu Ciller became the first female prime minister of Turkey in 1993.

More Reforms

One of the biggest changes Atatürk made was the creation of a new Turkish alphabet. Turkish became the required language for education, business, religion, and government. Atatürk dreamed of stamping out illiteracy.

To keep step with Europe, Turkey began using the 365-day Western calendar based on the earth's rotation around the sun. It had been using the Arab lunar calendar, which contains 354 days. Turkey also switched from the Islamic tradition of having Fridays off to having Saturdays and Sundays off. This gave Turkey and Western nations the same business week—Monday through Friday.

Atatürk died November 10, 1938. Due to his bravery and vision, Turkey emerged as an independent democratic nation. The next president was chosen by a peaceful election.

World War II

By the late 1930s, tensions had mounted in Europe. War seemed inevitable. President Ismet Pasha Inonu was determined to keep Turkey neutral. The president was also convinced that Adolf Hitler's German Army and supporting countries would not win the war. Turkey was not about to make the same mistake it did in World War I. Turkish leaders would not risk losing everything again. After August 1939, Turkish leaders signed a treaty offering to help Britain and France.

During the war, Turkey patrolled its waters and fly zone. They did not allow the German military or its allies to pass through Turkish-controlled areas. However, on June 18, 1941, Turkish leaders signed a treaty with Nazi Germany stating that both countries would not fight against each other.

Country Profile: Turkey

The BBC gives information on Turkey's leaders and media, as well as facts about Turkey and a basic overview of the country, at this Web site.

EDITOR'S CHOICE

Access this Web site from http://www.myreportlinks.com

By August 1944, Turkey broke off relations with Hitler's government. In February 1945, Turkey declared war on Germany. Turkey did this at least partially because it was a requirement to participate in the Conference on International Organization in April 1945. This conference resulted in the creation of the United Nations (UN). Turkey was voted in as one of the fifty-one original members in this world organization.

After World War II, Turkey and the United States developed closer ties.

Military Coup

As an infant republic, Turkey's democracy strained at the seams much of the time. A second political party was formed. Many people desired more private businesses, foreign investment, and freedom of the press.

In 1960, the two political parties' leaders could not agree in the assembly. Parliament reached a standstill. College students in Istanbul, military cadets, and other citizens violently protested. The military declared martial law.

On May 27, 1960, the Turkish Army arrested the president, the prime minister, and many parliament representatives. They were charged with disobeying the constitution and ruling without representation. The army also took control of government buildings and communication centers. New leaders assumed political power. They wrote a new constitution and created a so-called Second Republic. However, they stayed true to Atatürk's original principles.

Internal Unrest

In the 1980s, Turkey's economy was in horrible shape. Wages were low, and unemployment was high. The government could not even afford to import oil. During the winter of 1979 to 1980, people froze in their unheated apartments. Hospitals did not have power. People stood on long lines at stores for basic items such as lightbulbs, cooking oil, and salt.

By summer 1980, violence broke out in the city streets and countryside. Parliament came to a halt.

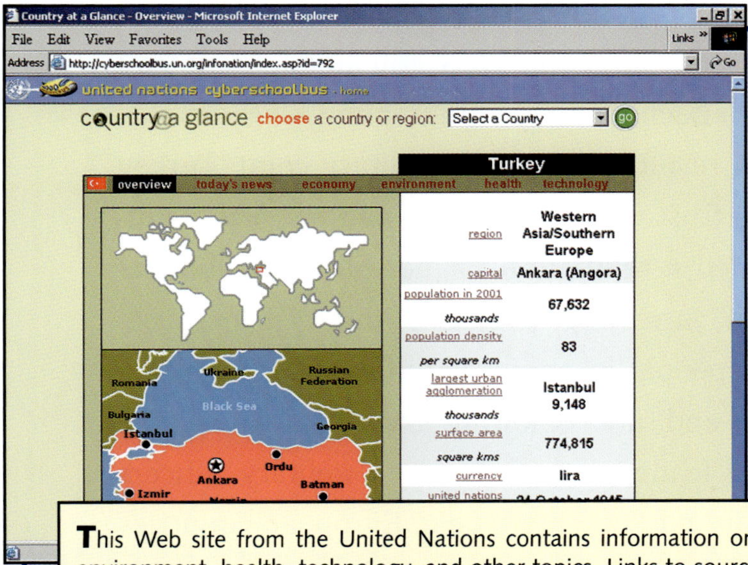

Country at a Glance: Turkey

This Web site from the United Nations contains information on Turkey's economy, environment, health, technology, and other topics. Links to sources for updated news are also provided.

Access this Web site from http://www.myreportlinks.com

The lawmakers could not agree to elect a new president. Extremist Muslims demanded Islamic law be brought back to replace civil law. On September 12, 1980, the military took control of the government for a second time. Military leaders installed their own cabinet members. They drafted a constitution based on France's constitution. This was declared Turkey's Third Republic.

The military enforced martial law. The Grand National Assembly was dissolved. The representatives were barred from running for office for ten years. Military officers did away with political parties. It became against the law for workers to strike for higher wages. The military arrested at least thirty thousand people. Two years later, tens of thousands of people were still jailed. Some had not even been charged with a crime.

As a result of the 1980 military coup, Turkey lost the trust of the European nations. The country gained a reputation for not allowing political freedom, arresting people without just cause, putting people in prison without trials, torturing people, and not honoring basic human rights. Western leaders asked Turkey's military officers to restore parliamentary rule. European countries stopped giving Turkey financial aid. In addition, the Council of Europe suspended the country's membership.

To gain European confidence, a new constitution declaring the Turkish government democratic and secular, was presented to the nation on July 17, 1982. Except for the areas heavily populated by Kurds, 91 percent of the people approved the new constitution. The following year's elections put an end to three years of military rule.

Seizing Cyprus

Cyprus sits as an emerald jewel in the blue Mediterranean Sea. It is a small island, one and a half times the size of Delaware. Cyprus is tucked under Turkey. Most of the citizens of the independent Republic of Cyprus, called Cypriots, are not Turks, but Greeks.

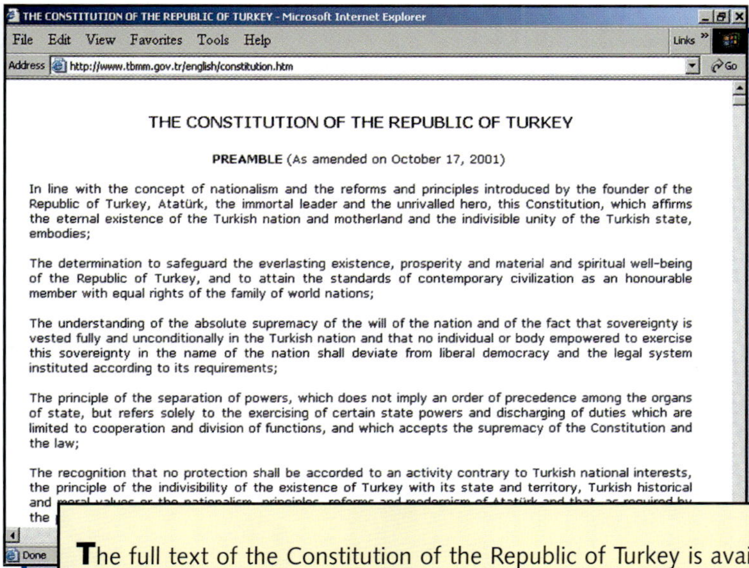
THE CONSTITUTION OF THE REPUBLIC OF TURKEY - Microsoft Internet Explorer

File Edit View Favorites Tools Help

Address http://www.tbmm.gov.tr/english/constitution.htm

THE CONSTITUTION OF THE REPUBLIC OF TURKEY

PREAMBLE (As amended on October 17, 2001)

In line with the concept of nationalism and the reforms and principles introduced by the founder of the Republic of Turkey, Atatürk, the immortal leader and the unrivalled hero, this Constitution, which affirms the eternal existence of the Turkish nation and motherland and the indivisible unity of the Turkish state, embodies;

The determination to safeguard the everlasting existence, prosperity and material and spiritual well-being of the Republic of Turkey, and to attain the standards of contemporary civilization as an honourable member with equal rights of the family of world nations;

The understanding of the absolute supremacy of the will of the nation and of the fact that sovereignty is vested fully and unconditionally in the Turkish nation and that no individual or body empowered to exercise this sovereignty in the name of the nation shall deviate from liberal democracy and the legal system instituted according to its requirements;

The principle of the separation of powers, which does not imply an order of precedence among the organs of state, but refers solely to the exercising of certain state powers and discharging of duties which are limited to cooperation and division of functions, and which accepts the supremacy of the Constitution and the law;

The recognition that no protection shall be accorded to an activity contrary to Turkish national interests, the principle of the indivisibility of the existence of Turkey with its state and territory, Turkish historical and

the

Done

The Constitution of the Republic of Turkey

The full text of the Constitution of the Republic of Turkey is available to read on this Web site.

Access this Web site from http://www.myreportlinks.com

Cyprus was a British Crown Colony until 1960 when it gained its independence. Fighting between Greek and Turkish Cypriots led to a coup to unite the island with Greece in 1974. The Turkish military intervened and has been stationed there ever since. On the divided island, 37 percent of Cyprus's northern tip is guarded by thirty-six thousand Turkish troops.

Turkish Cypriots declared themselves a separate state on November 15, 1983. Three days later, the United Nations Security Council signed a paper making this action illegal. The UN called for Turkish troops to withdraw from Cyprus. The military did not leave. No government in the

A female Cypriot does laundry at a Turkish Cypriot refugee camp in Hamitkoy, Cyprus, in 1964.

world except Turkey recognizes the "Turkish Republic of Northern Cyprus."

Kurds

Most Kurds are sheepherders and goatherders in the Taurus Mountains. This ethnic group lives in what they call Kurdistan, an area consisting of parts of Turkey, Iran, Iraq, Syria, and the former

Soviet Union. The Kurds have fought with these countries to make Kurdistan a separate and independent nation. As of 1999, fighting with the Kurds has killed more than thirty-five thousand people in Turkey alone.[7] It is estimated that there are anywhere from 330,000 to 2 million Kurdish refugees displaced due to war.

Road to a Stable Republic

In 1952, Turkey joined the North Atlantic Treaty Organization (NATO). NATO is an organization intent on keeping countries free from communism. Turkey has the second largest military in NATO after that of the United States.

Turkey on the Spot

Time magazine's Web site provides three articles dealing with the most recent elections in Turkey.

Access this Web site from http://www.myreportlinks.com

During the Cold War, Turkey supported the United States. It sent troops to Korea from 1950 to 1953 to serve with United Nations forces.

In summer 1990, Iraq invaded Kuwait. Turkey immediately supported United Nations sanctions against Iraq. The Turkish government stopped the flow of oil in a pipeline from Iraq to the Mediterranean coast. The assembly voted to allow foreign troops on Turkish soil. Turkey's military also served in the Persian Gulf War. The country gave permission to the United States Air Force to use the air base at Incirlik. The United States Air Force launched bombing raids from the Turkish base against Iraq during Desert Storm. As a result, the United States has continued to be supportive of Turkey.

During the past decade of a fairly stable government in Turkey, the emphasis has been to build roads and bridges and to improve services to the country's villages. But one of the country's biggest concerns has been to build a healthy economy. As Turkey entered the twenty-first century, Atatürk's words still rang true: Turkey has a lot of catching up to do.

Chapter 7 ▶

Economy

Agriculture has always been an important part of the Turkish economy. In 2004, it employed more than 35 percent of the country's population. However, manufacturing has become increasingly important since 1950. Like the agriculture industry, the textile industry employs about one third of the country's population.

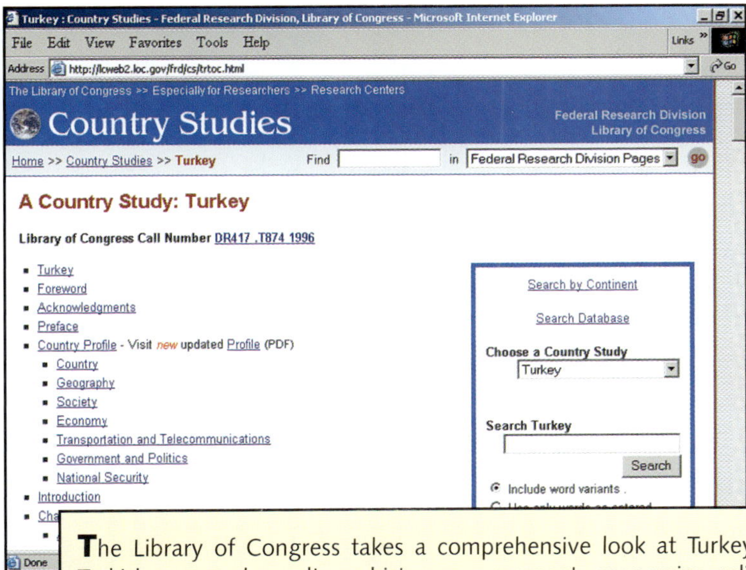

A Country Study: Turkey

The Library of Congress takes a comprehensive look at Turkey. Information about Turkish geography, culture, history, government, economics, religion, language, and other subjects can be found here.

Access this Web site from http://www.myreportlinks.com

Cereal Crops

Turkey has long been able to feed all of its people and still have leftover food to sell abroad. It exported $19 billion of food between 1994 and 2001. That is more than $2 billion of exported food each year.

Bread is the staple of life in Turkey. Farmers harvest 14 million to 20 million tons of wheat each year. People in Turkey eat more bread than most other people in the world.[1] Besides bread, this hard wheat makes excellent pasta.

Barley, rye, millet, corn, and rice make up other cereal crops grown in Turkey. Much of the barley, millet, and corn are grown for animal feed.

Cotton, Oils

Cotton is another major export. Fabric is made from cotton fibers. The cotton seed is used for vegetable oil. Most cotton in Turkey is grown on the south and southwestern coastal plains.

There are plenty of sunflowers and olive groves in Turkey, but oil from both is imported.

Tobacco

Tobacco has long been an exported crop. However, Europeans prefer tobacco grown in the United States. For this reason, it is unlikely that the Turkish tobacco industry will expand beyond the several hundred tons it is already growing without the aid of foreign investment.[2]

Hazelnuts

If you drive into the Black Sea coastal town of Giresun, you will see a sign that reads "Hazelnut Capital." Turkey is a major producer of hazelnuts. The country exports half a million tons of hazelnuts each year.

Other Crops

Turkey is the biggest producer of beans, lentils, and peas in the Middle East. Farmers also grow potatoes, sugar beets, grapes, raisins, citrus fruits, melons, and flowers. Irrigation, fertilizers, tractors,

Turkey has been exporting hazelnuts to foreign markets for six hundred years, and the country currently produces approximately 75 percent of the world's supply of the nut. Four million people in Turkey are in some way involved in hazelnut production.

and improved seeds have helped farmers grow larger amounts of healthier crops.

One crop you would not expect the government to be growing is poppies. But it does. The Turkish government strictly regulates poppy fields so the crop will not be used to make opium, an illegal drug. Poppies grown on the Anatolian plain are used for food, horse and cattle feed, and thatch roofs. The milky sap found in the unripe seed pods also makes medicines such as codeine and morphine.

Fishing

Although Turkey is surrounded by water on three sides, fishing is not a big industry for Turks. The Black Sea and Sea of Marmara contain the most commercial fishing beds. Frogs' legs, snails, shrimp, and crayfish are exported to Europe.

Livestock

War causes shortages and embargoes, even of food. As a result, live animals from Turkey have been known to be smuggled over the border to other Middle Eastern countries. Livestock provides meat, milk, eggs, wool, and hides for people.

Sheep and cattle graze mainly on the Anatolia plains. A variety of breeds of sheep are raised for different purposes. Turkish sheep are sheared of their coarse wool, which is used for carpets and blankets. Merino sheep grow finer, softer wool used for clothing. Merino sheep are mostly raised in the

A fisherman sells fish from his boat in Istanbul.

Bursa region. Mohair and angora, used in sweaters, are sheared from mountain goats.

One chicken farmer in Izmir claims to be one of the largest poultry producers in the world. However, most poultry farmers in Turkey own small businesses. They raise only five thousand to ten thousand fowl at a time. Much of the poultry is exported to Iran and Iraq.[3]

Automobile Industry

Manufactured goods are very important to Turkey's economy. In 2004, the nation exported

$64 billion worth of goods, $59 billion of which were manufactured goods, such as textiles, appliances, and cars. Nine automobile manufacturers, including Ford and General Motors, have plants in Turkey. Turkish workers make almost every kind of auto part. Workers at select plants in Bursa, Istanbul, Kocaeli, and Izmir assemble the cars.

The United States firm General Dynamics has a plant in Turkey that builds F-16 fighter aircraft.

Textiles

Turkey's largest manufacturing industry is textiles. The textile industry employed 33 percent of Turkish workers in the mid-1990s.[4] If the garment you are wearing was not sewn in Turkey, it could be that the cotton, silk, or sheep's wool was grown in Turkey. If so, Turkish weavers wove the fabric from which your T-shirt or sweater or cargo pants are made. For example, Land's End is one American company that buys fabric and clothing made in the Middle East and Asia.

Besides using cotton and wool, Turks make fabric and clothes from synthetic materials.

Leather goods are also exported from Turkey.

Services, Tourism

The services industry accounts for half of people employed in Turkey. Services include anything from banking to restaurants.

Tourism is an important service industry. Tourists vacation in Turkey to swim, sail, and sunbathe. People also tour historic, religious, and archaeological sites.

Germans top the list as one third of vacationers to Turkey. Russians are second. One and a half million Russian "snowbirds" flock to Turkey during their winter months. Germans and Russians prefer the warm Mediterranean coast. A million

Many visitors to Turkey like to relax on the nation's beautiful beaches. Here, tourists enjoy the public beach in the village of Kudasi on Turkey's Aegean coast.

British citizens vacation in Turkey each year. They prefer the Aegean coast.

Tourists from Western Europe, Israel, and the United States spend their vacations taking in the historic sites. They also relax on the beaches. Those from Iran and other Middle Eastern countries visit Turkey mainly to shop, usually in Istanbul and Bursa.

Tourism is a multibillion dollar industry. However, the number of tourists goes up and down depending on the situation in the Middle East. When there are wars or rumors of wars and unrest, people stay away.[5]

Natural Resources

The mining industry makes up only about 2 percent of Turkey's gross national product (GNP). Turkey's most important minerals are chromite, bauxite, and copper. Iron, manganese, lead, zinc, antimony, asbestos, pyrites, sulfur, mercury, and manganese are also mined. Many of these raw materials are used to make iron, steel, aluminum, cement, and fertilizers.

Energy

Turkey is not oil rich like its Middle Eastern neighbors. Turkey imports more than 23 million tons of oil and gas each year. What few oil fields can be tapped are in the Anatolian southeast borders by Syria, Iran, and Iraq. Oil is also located beneath the Aegean Sea; however, it is not currently being drilled for there.

Turkey acts as a pipeline highway for transporting natural gas from neighboring countries. An Iranian pipeline runs across the east Anatolian plateau. Italy built a pipeline that is buried under the Black Sea. Another pipeline transports crude oil from Azerbaijan to the Mediterranean Sea.

In times of war or bad relations with governments, Turkey has shut down the transport of gas and oil.

Sources of Power

By the mid-1990s, no village in Turkey was without electricity. Coal and hydroelectricity are the main sources of electric power. Hydroelectricity is electrical power generated by water. Turkish engineers dammed up the Tigris and Euphrates rivers to build hydroelectric plants. Many people, especially those in the country's rural areas, use manure and wood for fuel at home.[6]

Economic Future

Turkey has advanced economically since becoming a republic. However, it still lags behind Europe in this respect. It has less industry than European nations. In addition, Turkey is billions of dollars in debt and has high unemployment and low wages. It is important that Turkey catch up with Europe because the country wishes to join the European

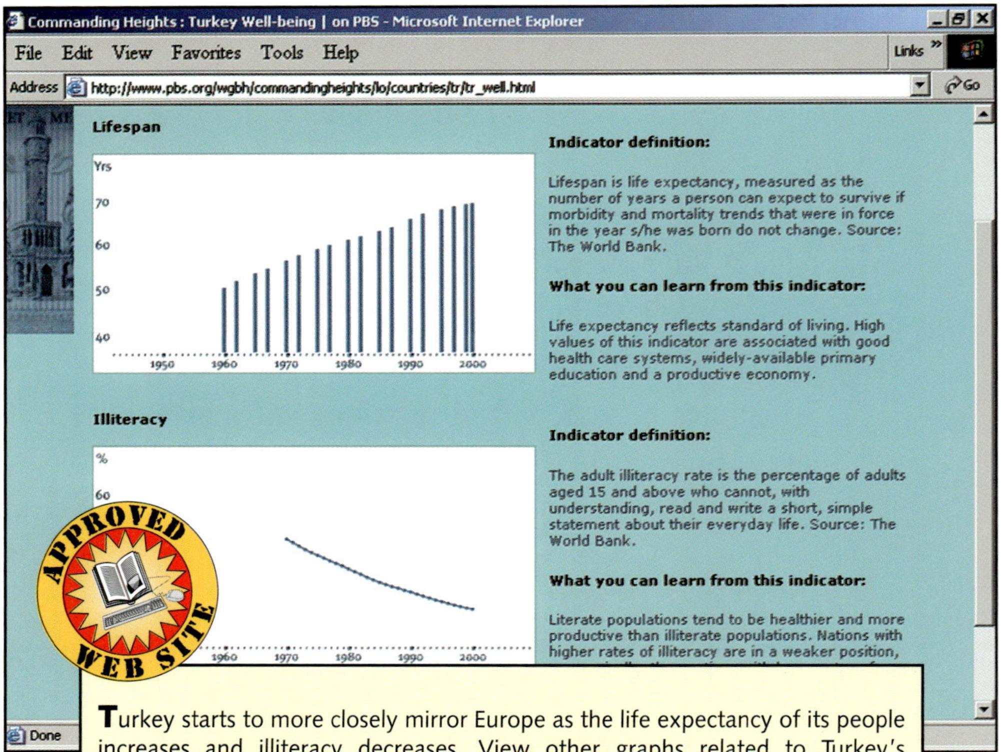

Turkey starts to more closely mirror Europe as the life expectancy of its people increases and illiteracy decreases. View other graphs related to Turkey's economy at the **Commanding Heights: Turkey** Web site.

Union (EU), the world's largest trading bloc. The Turkish government hopes that by joining the European Union, Turkey will be able to attract more industry. This will help to bring Turkey up to a European standard of living.

Chapter 8 ▶

Challenges of the Future

As in the past, Turkey gets pulled into Western and Eastern politics and disputes. Europe wants Turkey's government to be more like Western democracies. Yet Islamic Middle Eastern and North African nations do not want Turkey to turn away from its Muslim heritage. This tug-of-war has created many challenges for Turkey in the twenty-first century.

European Union

Twenty-five nations banded together to work toward common political, economic, and social goals. The European Union forms the world's largest trading bloc. Like a private club, nations have to qualify to become members. They have to be a democracy and financially stable. Twelve of the earliest nations in the European Union adopted the same monetary unit. It is called the euro.

Most Turkish people want to join the European Union. They believe if they become a member it will drive the Turkish government to adopt greater democratic freedoms. They also hope to gain financially. The European Union would

The euro has been in circulation since January 1, 2002. There are many economic benefits to adopting the euro as a nation's currency. These include stable prices for goods and services, low interest rates, and protection from economic fluctuations in non-European countries.

increase foreign investments from the West. This would help Turkey's economy.

The European Union formed in November 1993. Turkey did not become a candidate for membership until December 1999. From the beginning, the United States has supported Turkey becoming a full member. In November 1999, then-President Bill Clinton stated, "I feel very strongly that one of the . . . key questions to the future of this whole part of the world is whether Turkey is a full partner with the European Union. So I will continue to advocate it."[1] On October 3, 2005, the EU formally began membership talks with Turkey. The process is expected to take at least ten years.

European Union Requirements for Turkey

It has not been an easy road for Turkey to qualify for membership. The European Union nations demanded Turkey make thousands of changes in its penal code. There were five major areas where the European Union said Turkey needed to be more democratic:

- Turkey's laws must not limit free speech.
- The Turkish government needs to grant every citizen the right to express his or her own culture.
- The military should be under civilian control.
- Turkey must settle social conflicts by peaceful discussions and compromise.

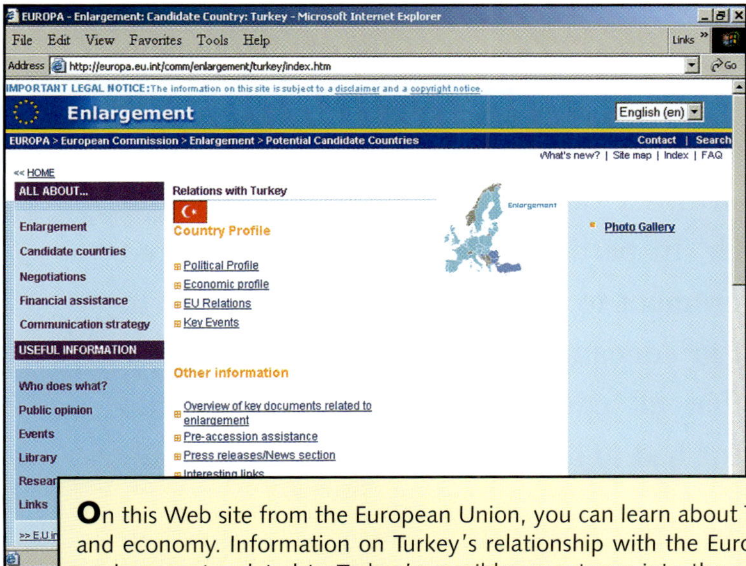

Relations With Turkey

On this Web site from the European Union, you can learn about Turkey's government and economy. Information on Turkey's relationship with the European Union, as well as documents related to Turkey's possible acceptance into the organization, can also be found.

EDITOR'S CHOICE

Access this Web site from http://www.myreportlinks.com

- Citizens should be given freedom to practice their religions as they think is right.[2]

Changes

Before Iraq's elections on January 30, 2005, Turkey was the only Muslim country in the world governed by a secular democracy. Although, by Western standards, its democracy is limited. As a young democracy, Turkey continues to limit civic freedoms. Turkey's leaders and citizens know they must change. The laws must be more democratic for all people, not just Turkish Islamic men. If not, Turkey will not get the prize of becoming a member in the European Union.

Turkey's leaders have been determined to make changes to meet the European Union's standards. In spring 2000, the Turkish parliament elected a president who spoke out for change. President Ahmet Necdet Sezer challenged the parliament to strike out all laws that limited freedom of speech. In particular, President Sezer wanted the government to allow the Kurdish language to be used in education and broadcasting. The law stated that all education, television, and radio broadcasts had to be in the Turkish language only.

Rising to the Challenge

Turkey has to prove it can be a successful democracy. It is not easy to change traditions overnight that have existed for centuries. Yet progress is being made. United States President George W. Bush said at a EU conference in 2004, "[Turkey is a] proud nation that successfully blends a European identity with Islamic traditions."[3]

On September 26, 2004, Turkey's parliament passed a massive penal code. The new laws made taxes fairer for all citizens. The military's influence has been reduced in government. The law did away with torture and the death penalty. Kurds gained rights to practice their own culture. Women are supposed to be treated more equally and will be protected after sex crimes.

Turkey has a long history of limiting freedoms and a poor human rights record. The true test will be

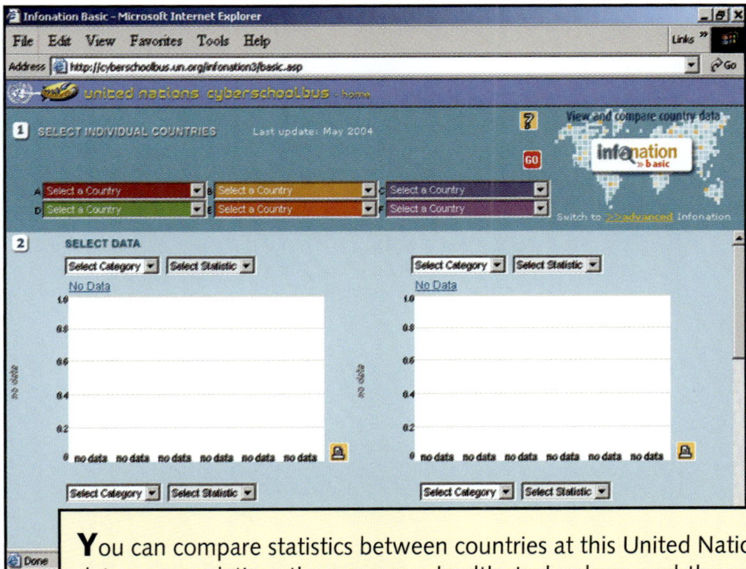

InfoNation Basic

You can compare statistics between countries at this United Nations Web site. Look at data on population, the economy, health, technology, and the environment for up to six countries at a time.

Access this Web site from http://www.myreportlinks.com

if Turkish judges, police, military, and government officials can follow the new laws. Even if Turkey does change enough to be eligible for EU membership, all current members still may not vote to accept Turkey into the European Union. France is the biggest opponent of Turkey being accepted. French leaders object to Turkey joining because its Muslim population may clash with the EU's Christian roots.[4] In Pope Benedict XVI's April 2005 acceptance speech, he spoke out against Turkey being allowed into the European

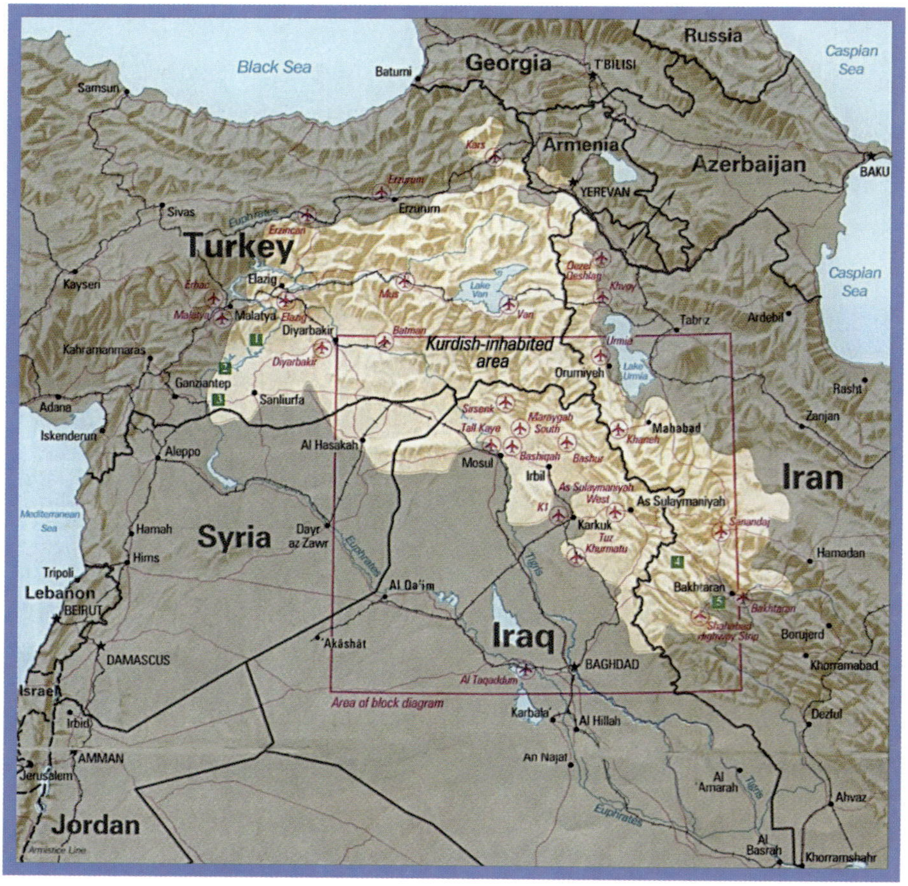

A map of Kurdish populations within Turkey and surrounding nations.

Union. The pope's reason was because Turkey is a Muslim nation.

A Divided Cyprus

The United Nations put together a plan to unify the two governments on Cyprus. The Turkish Cypriots accepted the UN plan. Greek Cypriots refused it.

On May 1, 2005, the European Union voted only the Greek Republic of Cyprus in as a member.

Kurdish Issue

Turkish leaders are worried that world powers, such as the United States and the United Nations, might give Kurds an independent Kurdistan. The European Union has put pressure on the Turkish government to give Kurdish citizens full rights under the law. The Turkish penal code passed in 2004 moved in this direction.

Peacekeepers Under NATO

The Taliban was removed from power in Afghanistan in 2001. In June 2002, Turkey became the lead nation of the International Security Assistance Force. Turkish troops were sent to help the Afghan government keep the peace in the capital, Kabul, and surrounding areas. The North Atlantic Treaty Organization took over the peace-keeping operation in August 2003. Turkey continues to supply troops to Afghanistan as part of a security force under NATO.

In a letter to Turkish Prime Minister Bulent Ecevit written in 2002, U.S. President George W. Bush wrote: "Turkey's participation and leadership in the war on terrorism deepens our countries' strategic partnership and provides Muslims around the world a hopeful model of a modern and secular democracy."[5]

Although the United States and Turkey have had a strained relationship since the beginning of the war in Iraq, the two nations share common economic and political goals. First Lady Laura Bush, Turkish president Ahmet Necdet Sezer, President George W. Bush, and Turkish first lady Semra Sezer (left to right) pose outside Cankaya Palace in Ankara, Turkey, on June 27, 2004.

American Military Presence

The United States uses two military bases in Turkey. Since 1947, the United States has given Turkey more than $14 billion in military aid. However, in 2003, Turkish officials would not allow the United States military to invade Iraq through northern Turkey. The United States coalition's war with Iraq strained relationships between the two countries.

Turkey-United States Relations

Turkey and the United States focus their relationship on areas such as energy supplies, trade, and investments. The two nations also fight together against terrorism. They share a common goal of making the Middle East region stable.

In 2005, U.S. Undersecretary of Defense Douglas Feith promised that ties would remain strong between the United States and Turkey. He said the United States military wants to use a key base in southern Turkey. This base is used as a cargo center for United States forces.

Turkey wants a good relationship with the United States for the same reasons it wants to be a member of the European Union: Turkey wishes to advance economically, politically, and socially. Because of Turkey's key geographical position and its commitment to democracy, the United States also relies on Turkey's people to be its friend.

Report Links

The Internet sites described below can be accessed at http://www.myreportlinks.com

Republic of Turkey
Editor's Choice Learn about Turkey's history, economy, government, and more.

Country Profile: Turkey
Editor's Choice Examine a profile of Turkey.

Turkey Observer
Editor's Choice Read the latest news from the Turkey Observer.

Relations With Turkey
Editor's Choice Get information on Turkey and its bid for EU membership.

Perry-Castañeda Library Map Collection: Turkey Maps
Editor's Choice View present-day and historical maps of Turkey.

Ministry of Culture and Tourism
Editor's Choice Learn about the culture of Turkey.

All About Turkey: Islam
Learn about Islam and its role in Turkish society.

The Ancient Theatre Archive: The Ancient Theatre at Aspendos
Take a tour of an ancient Turkish theater.

Background Note: Turkey
The U.S. Department of State provides information on Turkey's politics and economy.

BBC News: Middle East
Get the latest news from the Middle East.

The British Museum: COMPASS Collections Online
View artifacts from various time periods in Turkey's history.

Commanding Heights: Turkey
This PBS Web site will help you to better understand Turkey's history and economy.

The Constitution of the Republic of Turkey
Read the text of Turkey's constitution.

Country at a Glance: Turkey
Information on Turkey from the United Nations.

A Country Study: Turkey
The Library of Congress Web site contains an overview of Turkey.

Report Links

The Internet sites described below can be accessed at http://www.myreportlinks.com

Explore Istanbul
Read about Istanbul, an important city throughout history.

FIFA World Cup: Germany 2006: Turkey
Follow Turkey's national soccer team and its quest to win the 2006 World Cup.

Historic Figures: Alexander III of Macedon (356–323 B.C.)
Alexander III of Macedon played an important role in Turkish history.

InfoNation Basic
The United Nations provides statistics on countries around the world.

Ministry of Foreign Affairs: Diplomatic Archives: Turkish Presidents
On this Web site you can find a listing of all the presidents in Turkey's history.

Mustafa Kemal Atatürk: 1881–1938
Read about the founder of modern Turkey.

The 100 Most Useful Turkish Words
Learn important words to know while traveling in Turkey.

The Ottomans
Get an overview of the Ottoman Empire.

Turkey in Maps
View a collection of historical maps from the region we now know as Turkey.

Turkey in Pictures
Look at images from all over Turkey.

Turkey on the Spot
Find out why the elections of 2002 were important for Turkey's entrance into the EU.

Turkey Welcomes You
The official tourism Web site for Turkey contains useful information for the traveler.

Turkish Odyssey: History
Learn about the history of Turkey and the region.

The UnMuseum: Temple of Artemis
Read about the most famous shrine to Artemis, the fertility goddess.

***The World Factbook*: Turkey**
Learn more about Turkey from this CIA Web site.

al-Qaeda—An anti-Western terrorist network that is responsible for thousands of deaths worldwide.

bar mitzvah—A solemn and holy ceremony where a young Jewish male is initiated into his religious community as an adult.

caliph—The highest Muslim religious leader.

civil marriage—A marriage performed by a government official rather than a member of the clergy.

gazis—Turkish warriors hired to protect the territories of the caliphate.

gross national product (GNP)—The total value of goods and services produced by a country in a specific year.

hijra—Literally means "departure." For Muslims, this date is the first year of their calendar.

hydroelectricity—Electricity generated when water is used to spin a turbine.

Imam—A political leader and religious guide who Muslims believe is guided by Allah (God). Shi'ites believe Imams are only supposed to be descendants of Ali, Muhammad's brother-in-law.

jereed—A traditional Turkish horse-riding game dating back to when the Turks journeyed from Central Asia to Anatolia. Also known as çavgan.

jihad—"To struggle." The Qur'an teaches that a person who is oppressed wrongly can defend himself. The Qur'an teaches that if anyone dies in a jihad he will automatically go to paradise.

mujahid—A person who engages in jihad, or a "struggler for Allah."

minarets—Tall, slender towers that surround the mosque, a place of worship for Muslims.

mysticism—The ideas of a person who claims to have insight into mysteries beyond ordinary human knowledge. Often, mystics claim to have direct communication with a divine being, such as God.

parliament—A legislative body of government that makes laws.

penal code—Laws.

polytheism— The belief in or worship of more than one god.

recession—A period of significant decline in economic activity.

secular—Not religious or spiritual.

sultan—A Muslim leader who rules in political, military, judicial, social, and religious capacities. In theory, a sultan is responsible only to Allah and Allah's law.

trade embargo—A government order prohibiting trade with a specific country.

Venetian—A resident of Venice, located in present-day Italy.

Chapter Notes

Chapter 1. Terrorism in Turkey

1. "Standing in Istanbul," *Forward,* November 21, 2003, <http://www.forward.com/issues/2003/03.11.21/ed.html> (February 16, 2005).

2. Yigal Schleifer, "After bombings, Turkish Jews say community will try to remain open," *JTA Global News Service of the Jewish People,* November 17, 2003, <http://www.jta.org> (February 16, 2005).

3. "Standing in Istanbul," *Forward,* November 21, 2003, <http://www.forward.com/issues/2003/03.11.21/ed.html> (February 16, 2005).

4. "Islamic Terrorists Murder 24 in Turkey," *Israel News Agency,* November 15, 2003, <http://www.israelnewsagency.comturkey_jewish_terrorism.html> (February 14, 2005).

5. Jason Burke, Luke Harding, Helena Smith, "The Softest Target," *Observer,* November 23, 2003, <http://www.guardian.co.uk> (February 15, 2005).

6. Johanna McGeary, "When No One is Truly Safe," *Time,* December 1, 2003, p. 53.

7. Ibid., p. 54.

8. "The Islamic Great Eastern Raiders-Front," *Turks.US,* November 24, 2003, <http://www.turks.us> (February 14, 2005).

9. "Turkey Bombing Suspect Captured," *Associated Press,* December 19, 2003, <http://msnbc.msn.com> (February 14, 2005).

10. Jonathan Gorvett, "Call to Free Turk Bombing Suspect," *Aljazeera.net,* February 15, 2005, <http://english.alijazeera.net/NR/exeres> (February 15, 2005).

11. "Turkey Reviewing Terror Cell List," *CNN,* November 22, 2003, <http://edition.cnn.com/2003/WORLD/Europe/11/22/turkey.blast> (February 15, 2005).

12. James Helicke, "Turkey's Main Synagogue Reopens," *Associated Press,* October 12, 2004, <http://www.wwrn.org/parse.php?idd=34&c=162> (February 15, 2005).

Chapter 2. Land, Water, and Climate.

1. Helen Chapin Metz, ed., *Turkey: A Country Study* (Washington, D.C.: Federal Research Division, Library of Congress, 1996), p. 75.

2. Turkish Embassy at Washington, D.C., n.d., <http://www.turkishembassy.org> (February 1, 2005).

3. Metz, p. 77.

Chapter 3. Islam

1. Huston Smith, "Islam," John Miller and Aaron Kenedi, eds., *Inside Islam* (New York: Marlowe & Co., 2002), p. 26.

2. Ibid., p. 12.

3. Yahiya Emerick, *What Islam is all About* (Delhi, India: International Books of Islamic Literature, 1997), p. 164.

4. Akbar S. Ahmed, *Islam Today* (London: I.B. Tauris & Co. Ltd., 1999), p. 43.

5. "Islam," *Pearson Education,* 2005, <http://www.infoplease.com/ipa/A0001468.html> (August 31, 2005).

Chapter 4. Culture

1. "Language," *Turkish Ministry of Culture and Tourism,* n.d., <http://www.kultur.gov.tr/EN/BelgeGoster.aspx?17A16AE30572D313AAF6AA849816B2EFF8023BAEAB803944> (August 31, 2005).

2. Raymond G. Gordon, Jr., ed., *Ethnologue:*

Languages of the World, Fifteenth edition, (Dallas, Tex.: SLL International, 2005) as posted at *Ethnologue .com,* 2005, <http://www.ethnologue.com/show_country.asp?name=Turkey> (August 31, 2005).

3. Central Intelligence Agency, "Turkey," *The World Factbook*, November 1, 2005, <http://www.cia.gov/cia/publications/factbook/geos/tu.html> (November 22, 2005).

4. "The Women in Ottoman and Turkish Societies," *Turkish Cultural Foundation,* n.d., <http://www.turkishculture.org/lifestyles/women.html> (August 31, 2005).

5. Helen Chapin Metz, ed., T*urkey: A Country Study* (Washington, D.C.: Federal Research Division, Library of Congress, 1996), as posted at Library of Congress, *Country Studies,* n.d., <http://countrystudies.us/turkey.24.htm> (August 31, 2005).

6. "Kurds in Turkey," *Federation of American Scientists,* n.d., <http://www.fas.org/asmp/profiles/turkey_background_kurds.htm> (August 31, 2005).

7. Helen Chapin Metz, ed., *Turkey: A Country Study* (Washington, D.C.: Federal Research Division, Library of Congress, 1996), pp. 128–135.

8. Anna Zilboorg, *Fancy Feet: Traditional Knitting Patterns of Turkey* (Asheville, N.C.: Lark Books, 1994), pp. 8–9.

9. "Backgammon History," *Gammoned.com,* n.d., <http://www.gammoned.com/history.html> (August 31, 2005).

Chapter 5. Ancient Peoples

1. Helen Chapin Metz, ed., *Turkey: A Country Study* (Washington, D.C.: Federal Research Division, Library of Congress, 1996), p. 6.

2. Lloyd Seton, *Early Highland Peoples of Anatolia* (New York: McGraw-Hill, 1967), pp. 43–44.

3. Metz, p. 6.

4. Ibid., p. 9.

5. Ibid., p. 11.

6. Ibid., p. 14.

7. Jonathan Riley-Smith, ed., *The Oxford Illustrated History of the Crusades* (New York: Oxford University Press, 1995), p. 1.

Chapter 6. Twentieth-Century Turkey

1. Helen Chapin Metz, ed., *Turkey: A Country Study* (Washington, D.C.: Federal Research Division, Library of Congress, 1996), pp. 27–28.

2. Ibid., pp. 28–29.

3. Ibid., p. 30.

4. Ibid.

5. Ibid.

6. Stephen Kinzer, *Crescent and Star: Turkey Between Two Worlds* (New York: Farrar, Straus and Giroux, 2001), p. 41.

7. Elissa Haney, "Understanding the Turkey-Kurd Conflict," *Time Almanac 2004,* March 2, 1999 (updated since), <http://www.infoplease.com> (February 3–8, 2005).

Chapter 7. Economy

1. Helen Chapin Metz, ed., *Turkey: A Country Study* (Washington, D.C.: Federal Research Division, Library of Congress, 1996), p. 187.

2. Ibid., p. 189.

3. Ibid., p. 192.

4. Ibid., p. 206.

5. Andrew Mango, *The Turks Today* (Woodstock, N.Y.: The Overlook Press, Peter Mayer Publishers, Inc., 2004), p. 150.

6. Metz, p. 204.

Chapter 8. Challenges of the Future

1. "Remarks by the President and President Demirel of Turkey in Joint Press Availability," *William J. Clinton Foundation,* November 15, 1999, <http://www.clintonfoundation.org/legacy/111599-remarks-by-president-and-demirel-in-press-availability.htm> (October 7, 2005).

2. Stephen Kinzer, *Crescent and Star: Turkey Between Two Worlds* (New York: Farrar, Straus and Giroux, 2001), p. 175.

3. "Bush urges EU to let Turkey to Join," *AP/Government Custom Wire,* June 26, 2004, <http://0-web23.epnet.com.sapl.sat.lib.tx.us> (February 2, 2005).

4. Juliette Terzieff, "Why Turkey has become the Young Man of Europe," *San Francisco Chronicle,* January 23, 2005, <http://www.sfgate.com> (February 7, 2005).

5. "Afghanistan: Turkish ISAF troops settle in as lead nation," *United Nations Office for the Coordination of Humanitarian Affairs,* July 3, 2002, <http://www.irinnews.org/print.asp?ReportID=28617> (August 31, 2005).

Further Reading

Blomquist, Christopher. *A Primary Source Guide to Turkey.* New York: PowerKids Press, 2005.

Eboch, Chris. *Turkey.* San Diego, Calif.: Lucent Books, 2003.

Englar, Mary. *Turkey: A Question and Answer Book.* Mankato, Minn.: Capstone, 2005.

Halvorsen, Lisa. *Letters Home from Turkey.* Woodbridge, Conn.: Blackbirch Press, 2000.

Kemal, Neriman and Selina Kuo. *Turkey.* Milwaukee, Wisc.: Gareth Stevens Publishing, 2001.

Kneib, Martha. *Turkey: A Primary Source Cultural Guide.* New York: PowerPlus Books, 2003.

Mitten, Christopher. *Turkey.* Austin, Tex.: Raintree, 2002.

Orr, Tamra. *Turkey.* New York: Children's Press, 2003.

Pavlovic, Zoran. *Turkey.* New York.: Chelsea House Publishers, 2004.

Ruggiero, Adriane. *The Ottoman Empire.* Tarrytown, N.Y.: Benchmark Press, 2002.

Sheehan, Sean. *Turkey.* Tarrytown, N.Y.: Benchmark Press, 2004.

Wagner, Heather. *Turkey.* New York: Children's Press, 2002.

Index

A
Abdul Hamid II, 76–77, 78
Abu Bakr, 35
Adana, 47
Aegean region, 21, 23
Aegean Sea, 19, 21, 41, 103, 104, 105
  agriculture
  and economy, 97
  life of, 41
  regions for, 19, 21, 23
Agri Dagi. *See* Mount Ararat.
Ala Mountains, 20
Alexander the Great, 47, 48, 65
Alp Arslan, 68
al-Qaeda, 13–14
Anatolia, 7, 19
Anatolian Plateau, 23, 24, 25, 42
Anitkabir, 45
Ankara, 44, 55, 64, 66, 71, 85
Antakya, 47–48
Antioch. *See* Antakya.
Anti-Taurus Mountains, 19, 20
Arabian Platform, 25
Arcadius, 66
architecture, 48–50
Armenians in Turkish history, 64, 68, 80–81
Aspendos Theater, 49
Atatürk, Mustafa Kemal, 44, 45, 46, 82–88
automobile industry, 101–102

B
backgammon, 56–57, 58
bar mitzvah, 9
Beth Israel Synagogue, bombing of, 11, 16, 17
Black Sea, 18, 19, 21–22, 23, 41, 64, 99, 100, 105
Bosporus strait, 18–19, 42
British Embassy, bombing of, 11–13
Byzantine Empire in Turkish history, 66

C
calendar, 87–88
Cappadocia, 26
carpets, 51–52
Cave of Hira, 31
Central Anatolian Plateau, 20, 26
Central Anatolia region, 21, 23–25, 44
ceramics, 50–51
Ceyhan, 21
Christ Church, 15
Christianity, 27, 66
chronology, 7
Church of the Holy Cross, 81
Ciller, Tansu, 87
Cimmerians in Turkish history, 64
city life, 42–43
climate, 23–25
coal, 105
Cold War, 96
Committee of Union and Progress (CUP), 78, 80
Constantinople. *See* Istanbul.
Constitution of Medina, 32–33
constitutions, 76, 78, 80, 86, 90, 91, 92, 93
cotton, 98
the Crusades, 69–70
cuisine, 57–58
culture, 38
Cypriots. *See* Cyprus.
Cyprus, 92–94, 113

D
Dardanelles strait, 19
Dicle. *See* Tigris River.
dust storms, 24

E
earthquakes, 26, 47, 60
East Anatolia region, 21, 25
economy
  about, 97, 105–106, 108
  history of, 90–92, 96
  terrorism's effects on, 14–15
education, 40–41
Eid al-Adha. *See* Festival of Sacrifice.
Eid ul-Fitr. *See* Festival of Charity.
electricity, 105
energy, 104–105
Euphrates River, 20, 21, 59
euro, 107, 108
European Union, 105–110

F
family units, 41
Fertile Crescent, 21, 59–60
Festival of Charity, 36
Festival of Sacrifice, 36–37
fez, 86
Firat. *See* Euphrates River.
fishing, 100
France, 112

G
games, 54–57
Garden of Eden, 21
gazis, 7, 68, 70–72, 75
geography, 18–22
Germany in Turkish history, 80, 88–89
Göksu River, 21

government
about, 6, 37, 110
European Union requirements for, 109–112
history of, 78–96
reforms, 85–88
Grand National Assembly, 84, 91
Greeks in Turkish history, 61, 64, 83–84, 92–94

H

Hagia Sophia, 50, 73
hajj, 34–35
handicrafts, 52–53
Hat Act, 86
hazelnuts, 99
hijra, 32
history
early, 7, 44, 47, 59–77
of Islam, 29–34
modern, 78–96, 111–113
Hittites in Turkish history
artifacts by, 59
history of, 61–63, 64
peace agreements with, 7
settlements, 44, 47
HSBC, bombing of, 11–13, 15, 16
human rights, 90–92, 109–111
hydroelectricity, 105

I

Imam, 28, 37
industries, 101–104
International Security Assistance Force, 113
Iraq, 96, 114
Islam
about, 27–29
Five Pillars of, 34–35
history of, 29–34
Ismet Pasha Inonu, 88
Istanbul
commerce, 101, 102, 104
described, 42, 43–44
Hagia Sophia in, 50
history of, 66–73, 79, 82, 84, 90
Izmir, 44, 46–47, 83, 84, 101, 102

J

jereed, 54–55
jihad, 14, 32–34
Judaism, 27, 30

K

Kizil Irmak, 21
knitting, 52–53
Kocaeli, 25
Kurdistan, 94–95, 113
Kurds
described, 41, 47, 61, 94–95
history of, 81, 92, 111–113

L

lakes and rivers, facts about, 20–21
Lake Tuz, 20
Lake Van, 20, 25, 64, 68, 80, 81
languages, 6, 38–39, 48, 87, 110
literacy, 39, 40, 87
livestock, 100–101
locusts, 24

M

Maritsa River, 21, 84
Marmara region, 21, 22–23
martial law in Turkish history, 7, 90–92
Mecca, 28, 30, 34–35, 37, 73
Mediterranean region, 21, 25
Mediterranean Sea, 6, 19, 21, 22, 96, 103, 105
Mehmet II, 72–73
Mehmet V, 78
Mehmet VI, 82, 84
Meriç River. *See* Maritsa River.
military influence, 109, 111. *See also* martial law in Turkish history.
minaret, 27, 28
mining industry, 104
monetary unit, 6
Mongols in Turkish history, 71–72
monotheism, 31–32
Mountain of Light, 31
mountains, facts about, 6, 19–20. (*See also individual location by name.)*
Mount Ararat, 19, 26
Mount Erciyes, 26
Muhammad and Islam, 30–35
music, 54
musical instruments, 53–54

N

Neve Shalom Synagogue, bombing of, 9–11, 16, 17
Noah's ark, 19
North Anatolian Mountains. *See* Pontus Mountains.
North Atlantic Treaty Organization (NATO), 95, 113–114

O

oils, 98, 104–105
oil wrestling, 55–56

Ottoman Empire in Turkish history
and backgammon, 58
fall of, 79–82
and Hagia Sophia, 50
history of, 7, 70–77

P

Pasha, Ahmet Cemal, 80, 82
Pasha, Enver, 80, 81, 82
Pasha, Mehmet Talat, 80, 82
Pasha, Midhat, 76, 77
penal code, 109, 111, 113
Persian Empire in Turkish history, 64–65
Persian Gulf, 21
Persian Gulf War, 96
Phrygians in Turkish history, 63–64
pilgrimage, 34–35
Plains of Troy, 23
Pontus Mountains, 21, 23
poppies, 100
population statistics, 6, 18
poultry, 101

Q

Qur'an, 29, 32

R

rainfall statistics, 22
Ramadan, 34, 36
religion, 6, 37, 86. *See also* Christianity; Islam; Judaism.
rivers and lakes, facts about, 20–21
Romans in Turkish history
in Ankara, 44
in Antakya, 47
and Aspendos Theatre, 49
history of, 7, 64, 66–67
in Istanbul, 43
Rumi, Jalal ad-Din, 35
rural life, 41
Russia in Turkish history, 75, 80, 82

S

Sakarya, 21
Sea of Marmara, 19, 22, 100
Second Republic, 89–90
Selim I, 73
Seljuk Empire in Turkish history, 51, 67–69
services industry, 102
Seyhan, 21
Sezer, Ahmet Necdet, 110, 114
Shi'ites, 35
Smyrna. *See* Izmir.
soccer, 54, 55
Southeast Anatolia region, 25
sports, 54–57
Sufism. *See* Whirling Dervishes.
suicide bombers, 33–34
Süleyman the Magnificent, 73–74
Sultanahmet Mosque, 28
Sunnis, 35
synagogues, rebuilding of, 17

T

Taurus Mountains, 19, 25, 61, 94
Temple of Artemis, 48–49, 63
terrorism
about, 9–13
and economy, 14–15
suicide bombers, 33–34
suspects of, 13–14
war on, 113–115
textile industry, 102
Third Republic, 90–91
Tigris River, 20, 21, 59
tiles, 50–51
tobacco, 98
Torah on history, 29
tourism, 22, 25, 103–104
town life, 42–43
Treaty of Lausanne, 84
Treaty of Sèvres, 82
Troy, city of, 23, 24
Turkey
early peoples of, 59–61 *(See also individual civilization by name.)*
maps of, 5, 46
regions, 21 *(See also individual region by name.)*
Turkish knots, 52
Turkish language, 38–39, 87, 110

U

United Nations, 89, 93, 96
United States
relations with, 96, 114, 115
in Turkish history, 89

V

volcanoes, 26

W

War of Independence, 83–84
Whirling Dervishes, 35–36, 86
women
rights of, 87, 111
roles of, 37, 40, 52–53
World War I, 80, 81, 84
World War II, 88–89

Y

Yesil Irmak, 21
Young Ottoman Movement, 75–77
Young Turks, 77, 78, 79